HAUNTED
MEDINA COUNTY,
OHIO

HAUNTED
MEDINA COUNTY,
OHIO

BRANDON MASSULLO

Haunted
America

Published by Haunted America
A Division of The History Press
Charleston, SC
www.historypress.com

Front cover: Corkscrew Saloon, 2021. *Katrina Massullo.*

First published 2022

Manufactured in the United States

ISBN 9781467151481

Library of Congress Control Number: 2022936620

CONTENTS

PREFACE

Medina County is special to me. Not because I was born and raised here, but because I choose to live here. Throughout my life I've lived in several parts of Ohio and even the world, yet I feel most comfortable in Medina County. Perhaps it's the long walks with my dog at Leetha House Park in Spencer at sunrise, the casual conversations with the owner of Chatham General Store, the smiles and amazing muffins at Cool Beans Café, the cold beer and conversations at Lagerheads, concerts on the Medina Square or pulling up a barstool at the Village Inn in Chippewa Lake. Perhaps it's even simpler than that. Perhaps it's sitting by my pond watching the sunset, hanging out around the fire with friends or simply staring up at the clear country sky wondering about life… and the afterlife. Whatever the reason, Medina County is special to me.

How is Medina County special to you? What spaces or places shaped or molded you into the person you are today? In which school did you learn your ABCs? At which playground did you scrape your knee as a child? Where was your first kiss, house or speeding ticket? Where is your favorite spot to fish? We are shaped by the places and spaces that we frequent. Our personalities, beliefs, experiences and memories are tied to locations, places and spaces. Every place, space or location that I enter causes a reaction. Every space makes us feel a certain way, triggers certain memories, elicits beliefs and can even cause physical reactions (nausea, butterflies, etcetera). These emotional reactions could be happiness, sadness, fear, worry, hatred, joy, unease or myriad other feelings.

Tragedy, loss, fear and sorrow occur in places as well, and some believe that emotions tied to intense events are etched or imprinted on certain locations. Often when we think of ghosts or hauntings, it's the tragedies tied to a space that are most prominent. Have you ever sensed a presence or felt something brush up against you while alone? Heard or seen a ghost? Witnessed objects moving without cause? Experienced a sudden cold spot? Perhaps you have never experienced any ghostly phenomena, but you are enchanted by the possibilities of the afterlife. Whatever the case, I encourage you to embrace the extraordinary and remain open-minded as you read *Haunted Medina County, Ohio*.

ACKNOWLEDGEMENTS

I would like to express my sincere gratitude to the many people who provided me guidance and shared both their time and knowledge to make this book possible. I'm forever grateful to The History Press and Arcadia Publishing for providing me the opportunity to write this book. I would like to specifically thank my acquisitions editor, John Rodrigue, for his help and encouragement.

This book would not have been possible without the help of the wonderful staff and resources at the Medina County Library. Words cannot express my gratitude to Lisa Reinerth, who is a library associate at Medina County Library, for the contributions that she made to this book. Lisa is truly passionate about history, even the haunted kind, and her passion was responsible for uncovering several insights into the haunted lore of Medina County. It was Lisa's writing on local haunted locations that provided the inspiration and foundation for this book.

Mike McCann also provided valuable historical knowledge for several stories that are discussed in this book. Mike's extensive knowledge of Medina County's cemeteries and local resources was invaluable, and for that I am truly grateful. I'd also like to thank the owners and staff of certain local locations for taking the time to talk with me about the haunted history surrounding their establishments. Special thanks to Ken Collins, Laura Covey, Ryan and Mia Rose, Ryan and Brittany Marino, Rich Heileman, Tom Hillberg, Rod Knight, Leetha Mapes and Emma Schulte.

I would like to personally thank the Hinckley Historical Society, Lodi-Harrisville Historical Society, Liverpool Township Historical Society and Medina County Historical Society for allowing me to use their photos and taking the time to sit down and talk with me.

Thanks also goes out to my wife, Katrina, for her help with photographs for this book as well as her continued support. Behind every book that's written are supportive friends and family willing to allow the authors time to create and write. My interest in the paranormal and ghosts comes from supportive parents who were willing to allow me to make unorthodox decisions to pursue psychology and parapsychology.

Above all, I want thank the greatest storyteller I know: my dad, Alfred Massullo. I grew up in awe of his captivating stories. The greatest storytellers are not famous authors, actors or lecturers; rather, they are those blessed with the talent to captivate at a moment's notice, to inspire during a car ride to McDonald's, to teach lessons while in the waiting room of a dentist's office, to create an environment of wonder and astonishment when one is surrounded by fear and disappointment. Please take the time to thank the storytellers in your life.

INTRODUCTION

Around 150,000 years ago, Medina County was covered in ice estimated to be eight thousand feet thick. When it eventually receded and melted about 12,500 years ago, Medina County was left with one of Ohio's largest inland lakes (Chippewa Lake), rolling hills, valleys, rivers, swamps and caves that would give life to a wide array of plant and animal species. Joann King's wonderful book *Medina County: Coming of Age* points out that prehistoric people once roamed Medina County; spears and primitive tools that date to 10,000 BCE have been found in local fields. It's a bit surreal to think that prehistoric people once roamed, hunted and possibly lived in what is now my backyard.

The prehistoric age is fascinating; however, it's outside the scope of this book and, frankly, my expertise. As you can tell by its title, this book is not meant to be a comprehensive historical account of Medina County but rather a look into the haunted lore and ghostly phenomena that have been reported in Medina County. Since we are going to be diving into Medina County's most notable haunted buildings, restaurants, homes and cemeteries, perhaps we should fast-forward to the 1800s when the early settlers began to build these structures.

In 1803, Ohio became a state, and the first challenges early pioneers faced were clearing the dense forest, draining the swamps, addressing the wild animals, developing a government, surveying the land and making the land farmable. These tasks often resulted in death and tragedy due to illness, crime and the ferocious wildlife. In the early 1800s, Medina County was rampant with bears, wolves, panthers and wild hogs. Rattlesnakes up to eight feet long were also said to roam the wetlands. Along with these obstacles, early Ohio settlers also had to contend with two atrocities that even modern man knows all too well: squirrels and taxes.

According to the *Timeline of Medina County History*, the forests in Ohio were so dense in the early 1800s that it was said that "a squirrel could climb a tree in Cincinnati on the banks of the Ohio River, jump from tree to tree and make it to the shores of Lake Erie without ever touching the ground." As pioneers cleared trees, they faced the wrath of millions of angry squirrels, which destroyed crops and whole farming communities. These angry squirrels along with a property tax system that was confusing and unfair led to the state's first and only quick and decisive government resolution. In 1807, a law was passed requiring every male (of military age) to kill one hundred squirrels per year and deliver the hides to the township clerks when they paid their property taxes. The more squirrels killed, the higher the tax break. This seemed to solve both problems, until the government actually started to lose money as people brought in as many squirrels as they could— essentially paying their taxes with squirrels. If you are thinking about paying your taxes with squirrels this year, don't waste your time, as this law doesn't exist anymore. Again, please don't bring dead squirrels to the township clerk to pay taxes, as this will most likely result in jail time instead of a tax break.

While random settlers and Native Americans lived in the area in the early 1800s, Medina County wasn't officially organized until 1812. "Organized" is a relative term, in the sense that the land was given a name but remained attached to Portage County until there were enough voters to hold an election and form a government in 1818. The population in 1818 was 2,351, with the village of Wadsworth being the most populous. Harrisville and Liverpool townships were the first to be settled, and Homer township was last. Until 1840, Medina County included townships that are currently located in Summit and Lorain Counties (Norton, Copley, Bath, Richfield, Grafton, Sullivan, Penfield and Huntington). By the 1840s, many of Medina County's townships and villages were finalized to those we know today, and the dense forests filled with wildlife had become fields of grain, corn and other crops. Currently, Medina County consists of cities, townships and villages, which include Brunswick, Brunswick Hills, Chatham, Chippewa Lake, Gloria Glens Park, Granger, Guildford, Harrisville, Hinckley, Homer, Lafayette, Litchfield, Liverpool, Lodi, Montville, Medina, Seville, Sharon, Spencer, Wadsworth, Westfield Center, Westfield, Valley City and York. The 2019 census notes that Medina County currently has around 180,000 residents.

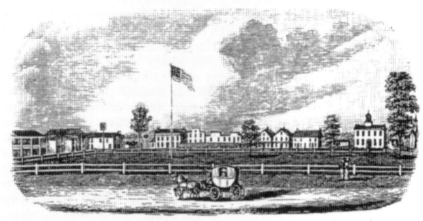

Drawn by Henry Howe in 1846.

PUBLIC SQUARE, MEDINA.

Medina Square illustration, 1846. *Courtesy of the Medina County Historical Society.*

If you picked up this book, I'm hoping that you are curious and opened-minded. Pompous historians and researchers are dismissive of the role that legends and lore play in history, often believing that if something can't be found in databases, land deeds, tax maps, newspaper accounts, historical texts, preserved letters, photographs, court proceedings or birth, marriage or death certificates, then to some extent it did not exist. Medina County's extensive history is well documented; however, there is also a hidden history that is found not in archives or databases but in stories and experiences passed down from generations. The hidden history I'm referring to isn't nefarious, nor does it only pertain to ghosts; "hidden" simply means nobody documented the experience. Below is an example of how I learned the most about my house in Medina through series of conversations with my neighbor, rather than combing through databases and land deeds.

A few moments after we pulled into our newly purchased house in Lafayette Township, our neighbor appeared. He was an older gentleman in his early nineties, wearing glasses and suspenders. He insisted that we come over to his house for a cup of coffee. Not wanting to be rude, I agreed; my wife, however, was too focused on the move and elected to stay back and get things organized. Before the coffee was even poured, he began to tell me the history of my property. "Forty years ago, I could sit at this very table and see Chippewa Lake as clear as I can see you." Over those forty years, his view had been obstructed by house development, neighbors planting trees and other modern changes. He showed me pictures of the construction of our pond, what the original tree line looked like and the people who built our home. He shared stories about previous owners, their children and even grandchildren. He felt obligated to educate me on the area and pass on his knowledge. Sadly, that neighbor died only a few years after we moved in. I'm an academic at heart; however, I understand that not all history comes from books, academic institutions, archives, databases, libraries, written records or the internet. History also comes from stories passed down from generation to generation. What I learned from my neighbor could not be found by combing through databases, archives or newspapers or by searching the internet. It was by engaging in conversations with older generations that I learned the most information about my home, information that would have been lost without the lived experience of interacting with others.

Our stories and lives are not a collection of legal documents. My paternal grandfather died in 1994, and if you research him through various internet and library resources, you will find his birth certificate, military records, various addresses and death certificate and a list of his relatives. However, this is not an accurate portrayal of my grandfather; rather, it is a dull collection of meaningless facts. The true history of my grandfather is only conveyed through stories told by those who knew him. Information gathered through oral history can often be viewed as being subject to exaggeration and inaccuracies. Does this make the information gathered less valuable or important? I would argue that oral history is more important, as it fills in the blanks between birth, marriage and death certificates. Experiences, stories, legends and folklore are the aspects of history that fascinate me the most.

Folklore and stories of haunted houses are often the result of retelling experiences from the past. These stories are often a mixture of truth, exaggeration, legends and cultural beliefs. This book is not meant to convince anyone that ghosts exist or not; rather, I'm retelling the stories and legends of Medina County from generations past. Everyone has heard a ghost story, and many people have toured a house or location that is allegedly haunted. I never gave much thought to these stories when I was in high school; however, looking back at the mixture of history, folklore and paranormal phenomena surrounding those locations, I now find it to be fascinating.

If you asked one hundred people to define "ghost," the general consensus would most likely be that ghosts are simply the spirits or souls of those who have died. Inherent in this thought is the idea that humans have a soul and that our thoughts, personalities, interests, memories and dislikes are not biologically based and can live on after our physical body dies. This goes against modern science, which is pretty confident that our personal identity and behaviors are the result of nerve cells, molecules and brain processes. Mainstream science's view is disliked by many people, as it paints humans as robots and our emotions and identities as the result of our circuitry. Most disturbing for many is the fatality of mainstream science's view on death, which is simply that the machine stops working, similar to a TV, and with death, an individual's personal identity ceases to exist in any dimension. That's pretty depressing, huh? Individuals who are religious or spiritual view the soul as the invisible, incorporeal essence of a person, which survives death. A common Catholic belief is that at death, one's soul leaves the physical body and enters heaven or hell. Many other religions also have beliefs regarding the soul, such as reincarnation, which is essentially the transfer of the soul from one individual being to another.

Before we proceed, I want to clarify some terms. Throughout the book, I will use the terms *ghostly encounters*, *haunt-type phenomena* or *ghostly experiences*. These terms are essentially interchangeable and refer to experiences or commonly reported phenomena associated with ghosts, spirits and haunted locations, such as visual apparitions, the sense of a presence, auditory phenomena, dizziness/headache, objects moving, overwhelming feelings/emotions, unexplainable weakness of body parts, muscle pain, overwhelming fatigue, skin irritation, tactile phenomena, unusual lights/energy, change in temperature, tingling/burning sensations, nausea, unexplained pressure, and so forth. A ghostly encounter does not mean unequivocally that the witness saw an apparition. A ghostly encounter could be a sensed presence, a person feeling as if they were touched or a sudden and unexpected change in temperature.

I haven't investigated hundreds of haunted locations, nor do I own a vest with hundreds of pockets. I never understood why ghost hunters on TV always have those vests. I do not dress in all black. I don't claim to have psychic talents. I'm not part of a paranormal investigation team. What I am is extremely fascinated with reports of ghostly encounters. My passion has led to countless hours combing through the paranormal literature and speaking with people who report ghostly encounters. When someone is recalling their ghostly experience, their whole persona changes. You can physically see the rush of emotion and excitement on their faces. The people around them change as well. From staunch skeptics to steadfast believers, their ears perk up and their eyes widen when someone is recalling a ghostly encounter. Everyone is fascinated with ghosts.

Having a ghostly experience is often portrayed as being terrifying and frightening; however, this may only be a momentary reaction. In reality, having a ghostly encounter is beneficial for your overall health and wellness. Research has shown that individuals who reported at least one paranormal experience believed that these experiences increased their interest in spiritual matters and improved their overall sense of well-being. Along with indicating that their experiences resulted in increased happiness and confidence, they also reported a decreased dread of death, depression, loneliness and fear. The common assumption is that paranormal experiences such as hauntings are a cause of distress, but this appears to be a short-term reaction. TV programs tend to focus on the sensational or negative effects of hauntings, as their goal is to entertain. Imagine that you are at home and you encounter an apparition. For argument's sake, let's say that this experience is 100 percent authentic and even witnessed by another credible person. This experience would be, in my opinion, positively life changing. Not only would it confirm to you that ghosts exist, but it would also shed light on consciousness and life after death.

While reading other people's ghostly encounters, please try to keep an open mind. Discounting someone's personal experience is both closed-minded as well as an example of being a "poopy head." I know there are people in the audience that are skeptical of paranormal phenomena. Many may believe that these reported phenomena are the result of fraud, attention-seeking behaviors or even mental illness. My role here is not to try to convince anyone that ghosts, spirits or paranormal phenomena exist; rather, it is to acknowledge that millions of people each year report these ghostly phenomena, which warrants investigation. Those who seriously research paranormal phenomena are not asking "Do ghosts exist?" but rather "Do people experience ghosts?" The answer is yes, people experience ghosts; however, science doesn't really know what ghosts are. Ghosts may be discarnate entities, souls of the deceased, telepathy, brief glimpses of another dimension or simply unconscious tricks of our minds. Nobody can dispute that people report apparitions, so instead of arguing whether or not these experiences are ghosts, we should be focusing on trying to explain these phenomena. My viewpoint is to look at the reported ghostly phenomena on an individual basis. Does seeing an image of a deceased family member mean unequivocally that one has witnessed a ghost? It doesn't. There are numerous natural explanations for ghost sightings, such as magnetic fields, hallucination, misinterpretation, a dream state, etcetera. Even among believers, there can be different explanations, such as astral projections, past lives intruding on the present day, ESP, clairvoyance, etcetera.

In this book, I want to retell the paranormal experiences and legends associated with certain locations in Medina County. Another goal is to determine if there are any solid facts to the origins of these stories, spirits and legends. The last and final goal is to entertain. You don't have to travel to other countries, states or cities to visit haunted locations. Medina County has numerous locations that are said to house spirits. So sit back, grab your favorite beverage, turn the lights down and join me as we take a tour of *Haunted Medina County, Ohio*.

CHAPTER 1
MEDINA LIBRARY

Most everything at the Medina County Library is free—even the ghostly experiences. Full-torso apparitions, spirit knocks, phantom smells, mysterious electrical issues and book carts mysteriously flipping over are just some of the haunt-type phenomena reported by the library staff.

A meeting was held on January 15, 1877, in the upstairs room of Shepard's Dry Goods Store (currently Cool Beans Café) to discuss opening a library in the village of Medina. The meeting was organized by a Professor Cummings, who was the superintendent of Medina schools. At the meeting, the Medina Circulating Library Association was formed, with the sole purpose of bringing a library to the village. Their only problem was that they had no room and no money. Herbert H. Brainard solved these issues when he agreed to house the library's seventy books in his jewelry store (currently Laplaca Jewelers). At some point, the library was moved to another jewelry store on the square when a deal was struck with Miss Meroa Andrews, who owned and operated Andrews Jewelry (currently Chill Ice Cream). Miss Andrews would set up the library in a section of her store and become the village librarian for an annual salary of twenty-five dollars. At this point, the library had amassed five hundred books. Miss Andrews sold her store in 1899, and the library relocated to a small building on 103 North Public Square; Miss Eva Johnson become the new librarian.

In *Medina County: Coming of Age (1810–1900)*, Joann King notes that "at a time when Andrew Carnegie used his wealth to open free libraries across the land, the *Gazette* editor asked who was the rich man of Medina County who would step up and do the same?" The local newspaper essentially put a call out to the wealthy families of Medina County to finance the town's library. In 1904, Franklin Sylvester, who was a wealthy farmer and livestock raiser, made three generous donations totaling $15,000 (equivalent to $419,703 in today's money). In 1907, the Franklin Sylvester Library was opened on the corner of Washington and Broadway Streets. It contained over two thousand books. Mr. Sylvester donated the money on one condition, which was that the library always bear his name.

For seventy-five years, the library was the namesake of Mr. Sylvester, until the library board voted to change its name to Medina County Library in 1982. The library continued to honor the contributions of Mr. Sylvester by naming a room after him, which housed local research and genealogy materials until renovations in 2019 resulted in the Sylvester Room being removed. While the library is not officially named after Sylvester, nor is there any room dedicated to him, his name is still etched in the original 1907 building's entrance. I'm sure that the spirit of Franklin Sylvester understands that times change and so do names—right? Wrong.

It's suspected by some of the library staff that the ghost of Franklin Sylvester haunts the library, in large part because he is upset about the name changes and recent renovations. Reminds me of the old saying, "Hell hath no fury like a wealthy Medina farmer who donated money to build a library with the agreement that the library be named after him, only to have them change the name." I might be a little off with that saying. In all honesty, Mr. Sylvester, the library still has your named etched on the old entrance, so stop being such a baby… is something I will never utter in the library.

Franklin Sylvester (1831–1907) was born in Bristol, New York, on March 28, 1831. When he was two, his parents moved to Granger Township, where he would end up spending the rest of his life. The Sylvesters did not come from money and were described as poor and hardworking. Franklin was one of seven siblings and at the age of nine was hired out to a local Sharon farmer for three dollars per month. He worked tirelessly for six months and took the twenty-one dollars that he earned to buy his family a cow, which they desperately needed. He continued to complete farm labor, and at age sixteen, he bought a team of horses and took on hauling contracts. By age twenty, he had bought a farm and was raising cattle, amassing a small fortune. According to the June 7, 1907 edition of the *Medina Gazette*, by age thirty-five, he was known throughout Medina County as an "honest, trustworthy, successful cattle dealer, and a man whose word

Right: Opening of Sylvester Library, 1907. *Courtesy of the Medina County Historical Society.*

Below: Medina County Library, old building entrance, 2021. *Brandon Massullo.*

was a good as a bond." By the time of his death, he had accumulated close to 1,500 acres of land, which the *Medina Gazette* described as "the best land in Northern Ohio." Franklin Sylvester and his wife, Eunice Sylvester (1830–1935), never had children; however, they were known in the community for using their wealth to aid the youth of Medina. Mr. Sylvester was a tall man; the *Gazette* described him as a "strong man cast in a large mold." He had dark hair and often dressed in a solid black suit. Mr. Sylvester was a very prominent figure in Medina County who "typified all that was best and strongest in the life

Franklin Sylvester. *Courtesy of the Medina County Historical Society.*

of our rural community.…He was one of Medina's most notable and useful citizens."

One theme with Mr. Sylvester is that he prided himself on his self-reliance and honesty in life and business. Another theme is that he despised deceit and hypocrisy. According to the October 4, 1907 edition of the *Medina Gazette*, "When he liked a person, he was a true friend. He was ready and willing to aid any good cause, but he hated hypocrisy and deceit above all things." The *Gazette* reported that Sylvester "was never known to stoop to any underhanded work or deceit in his deals.…There was an unadulterated honesty and hatred of sham." During the opening dedication of the Franklin Sylvester Library, Joseph Andrew, who was a lifelong friend of Sylvester, stated, "When a man has accumulated a fortune honestly, without a stain on a single dollar of it, and sees fit to make a gift from that fortune that will benefit the present and future generations, he truly can be called a philanthropist." There was a call from the public in 1907 to commission a life-size portrait of Franklin Sylvester to hang in the library and a booklet telling his story, so that future generations would be aware of the contributions that he made to this county. Both of those things never occurred. If I have learned anything about Franklin Sylvester, it's that he took the saying "A deal is a deal" to heart in life. Is the same true in death? Is Mr. Sylvester's ghost upset that the library broke their deal and changed its name?

Prior to renovations in 2019, the Franklin Sylvester Room housed the county's local history resources and a portrait of Mr. Sylvester. Staff often reported sensing a presence when alone in this room. Upon entering the room, staff got into the habit of greeting Mr. Sylvester: "Good morning, Mr. Sylvester; hope you are doing well." "Good night, Mr. Sylvester." One morning, while opening the library, a staff member entered the room and greeted Mr. Sylvester as she had always done, and when she looked up—he was actually there. She witnessed a full-torso apparition of a man very similar to Mr. Sylvester's description in front of her in dark clothes. She politely smiled, turned around and walked out. Standing face-to-face with an apparition must be both terrifying and exciting. I often wonder if I would run away or try to communicate. What would you do?

In 2009, Lisa, a library staff member, and her coworker were sorting books that had been returned to the library. The sorted books are organized and placed in several carts to return to the shelves. Lisa recalls that while shelving the books, they heard a loud crash. They noticed that one of the carts was tipped over. The cart was not overloaded, and after inspection, they could not find any issue with the wheels. According to Lisa, "Seemed like somebody was upset and just pushed it over." Lisa states that anytime something unusual or spooky happens in the library, the staff says, "It's just Franklin."

Library staff member Kathy recalls an eerie occurrence as well:

A few years after I started here, after closing, several of us were sitting around the reference desk talking. It had been a very busy Monday night and we were kind of de-briefing....The rest of the staff had gone and locked up as they went. We were the only ones in the building. Then, the book elevator, which was not used because of the tendency to lose books down the crack between the elevator floor and the department floor, slowly came up and opened its door. Needless to say, there was no one in it.

According to library staff, activity ramped up during the recent renovations when the Franklin Sylvester Room was removed. At one point, Mr. Sylvester's portrait was taken off the wall and placed in a closet for safekeeping during construction, which could have angered him even more. In the summer of 2019, Lisa was reshelving DVDs in the library's second-floor DVD room when she noticed someone in dark clothing intently looking at one of the shelves. She turned her head momentarily to place a DVD on the shelf, and when she looked back, the man disappeared. Shocked, she headed to the entrance of the DVD room and asked a coworker sitting at the desk, "Did you see anyone leave here?" The coworker replied, "Nope." This ghostly encounter would have been the second sighting of a full-torso apparition

DVD room where apparition of Franklin Sylvester was seen, Medina Library, 2021. *Brandon Massullo.*

believed to resemble Mr. Sylvester. This certainly can't be a coincidence; however, three sightings would be more compelling. Lisa saw this same apparition of a tall man in dark clothing in the DVD room several months later. OK, this is getting very interesting.

While the library was closed during COVID-19 lockdown, one staff member was working alone stocking books in the nonfiction section (astronomy). All of a sudden, she was overcome with a very strong and distinct odor of men's cologne. Nobody else was in the building.

Mr. Sylvester is not the only ghost believed to roam the library. The spirits of two little girls have also been reported in the children's section on the first floor. The phenomena surrounding the girls are very playful and seem to be localized to the children's department. Children's laughter has been heard around closing time when no children are in the building. On one Saturday night, which was a full moon, a staff member in the Children's Department had a very unusual occurrence happen.

The elevator in the children's area would open and close on the first floor with no one entering or exiting it. It did this over fifteen times during the day. I would press the button to send it to another floor, and it would come back to floor one soon after and repeat the pattern. If there was a malfunction with the elevator, it would have been sent to the GROUND floor for fire safety issues. This was like a little kid was playing with the elevator…. At one point I said out loud, "We don't play on the elevator."…I walked up the stairs to the third floor and the elevator opened on the third floor. The elevator only goes to the third floor when a staff member's badge was scanned so I was convinced that my co-worker was playing a trick on me.….She assured me that she had not sent it to the third floor.

There is no question that there have been several reports of bizarre occurrences in the Medina County Library, so let's take a look further into the location's history. Clearly Franklin Sylvester has a link with the library, as he was the sole contributor to funding the construction of the building; however, Mr. Sylvester unfortunately died prior to the completion of the library and actually never set foot inside. No tragic death has ever been reported at the library, and without any specifics on the ghosts of the little girls, there is not much more to look into. The property the library was built on once consisted of several properties, which were either demolished or relocated to make way for the library. As the library expanded, it acquired and cleared more land that used to be businesses and residences. It would be a daunting task to explore all those properties and those who frequented them.

In the accounts of the ghostly phenomena reported at the library, there has been an underlying theme that Mr. Sylvester is angry; however, this may not be the case. If we're going to play the role of ghost psychologist, perhaps Mr. Sylvester's presence in the library is out of pride for the legacy he left behind. All of his 1,500 acres have been parceled off and sold, his cattle and livestock are long deceased and his other assets are lost to time; however, one part of him that has lived on for over 114 years is this library. As a matter of fact, in combing through the history books on Medina County, there is little mention of Mr. Sylvester. I like to think he shows up occasionally in the library to just soak in his legacy and perhaps to check in on the staff to make sure they are maintaining the books and resources in his building.

In talking with library staff and researching the ghostly encounters reported at the library, I found that the phenomena are not at all menacing or malicious. I would like to emphasize that simply being enchanted with the experiences is what makes haunt-type phenomena so fascinating, and the library has a lot of those.

CHAPTER 2
THE BRUNSWICK HILLS BATHROOM GHOST

There are strange and unusual noises coming from the men's restroom at Plum Creek Park in Brunswick Hills. These terrifying sounds are not the result of Taco Bell but rather the ghost of a teenage boy said to haunt the park's restroom. Of all the places and times to have a ghostly encounter, I would imagine in a bathroom, while "doing your business," would be the worst.

According to legend, a teenage boy, out late at night with his girlfriend, went to use the restroom. Upon entering the restroom, he was confronted by an ex-con and killed. After killing the boy, the ex-con was reported to have gone on a killing spree. It's said that in the "wee-wee" hours of the night you can hear the teenager's screams from the bathroom. Those who have entered, fearing someone was in danger, found the place empty, and when they attempted to leave the restroom, the building would violently and mysteriously shake.

As with most folklore and legends, there are no police reports to substantiate a murder in the restroom at Plum Creek Park; however, there is some truth to this tale…kind of. The story mentions an ex-convict killing a young man in a park in Ohio and then going on a serial killing spree. This actually occurred.

Edward Wayne Edwards is described as one of the most prominent serial killers in the world. The television network A&E aired a six-part true crime series, *It Was Him: The Many Murders of Ed Edwards*, in which a retired cold case detective stated he believed that Edwards killed up to one hundred

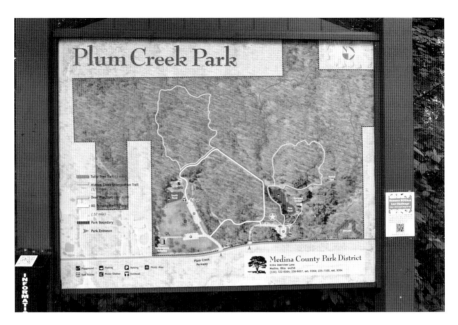

Plum Creek Park trail map. *Katrina Massullo.*

people and even suspected that Edwards could be the Zodiac Killer. To better understand how Edwards is linked to a men's restroom in Brunswick Hills, we have to delve a little deeper into his history.

Edward Wayne Edwards was born in Akron in 1933. After his mother's death in 1935, he was sent to an orphanage in Parma, Ohio, and then to a reform school in Pennsylvania. Edwards returned to Akron in 1950 and began committing burglaries. He joined the army for a couple years until he was dishonorably discharged. Throughout the '50s and '60s, Edwards was arrested several times for armed robbery and burglary. Edwards never wore a mask or concealed his identity because he wanted to be recognized and had a desire to be famous. He escaped from jail on two occasions, once in Akron in 1955 and once in Portland in 1960. Ultimately, he was caught and sentenced to sixteen years in Leavenworth Penitentiary in Pennsylvania. He was paroled in 1967 and, surprisingly, toured the country as a motivational speaker, discussing the positive impact of prison reform. He was a very popular and well-known ex-convict in the '70s, which led to appearances on the popular TV shows *To Tell the Truth* and *What's My Line?* In 1972, he wrote an autobiography titled *Metamorphosis of a Criminal: The True Life Story of Ed Edwards*. Unfortunately, he would soon return to a life of crime. He was charged with and convicted of arson in 1982. After spending four years in prison, he was released in 1986. In 2009, he was arrested and charged with the 1980 murders of Timothy Hack and Kelly Drew in Wisconsin. These murders were called the Sweetheart Slayings, as Timothy and Kelly were a teenage couple. While in prison, Edwards confessed to murdering a young couple in 1977 at Silver Creek Park in Norton, Ohio.

Silver Creek Park is located just thirty miles from Plum Creek Park. Not only are they close in distance, but they are also close in spelling (replace "Silver" with "Plum"). On August 8, 1977, the bodies of William "Billy" Lavaco, twenty-one, of Doylestown and Judith Straub, nineteen, of Sterling were found in Silver Creek Park. Both had died of gunshot wounds. The exact location of the murder at the park was not disclosed, nor was the motive. Edwards lived in Doylestown, Ohio, which is just outside of Medina County, from 1974 to 1978, and police believed that he knew one of the victims. The murders at Silver Creek Park occurred in 1977, after which Edwards is believed to have murdered the couple in Wisconsin (1980), a young man in Burton, Ohio (1996), and possibly many more. This would mean that after the killings in Silver Creek Park, this well-known ex-convict, Edward Wayne Edwards, went on a serial killing spree (this part lines up with our original ghost story). I want to be clear that there are no police reports of a murder at Plum Creek Park in Brunswick Hills. There are also no reports of ghosts at Silver Creek Park in Norton, Ohio. As with most folklore and ghost stories, the origins of the ghost of Plum Creek Park appear to be more fiction than fact. Perhaps this urban legend was created to scare teenage couples from venturing into parks after sunset or as a warning that unsavory individuals are hiding everywhere and anywhere in the darkness—even in restrooms.

CHAPTER 3
THE LADY IN BLUE

A small, well-maintained, unassuming white house sits at the intersection of Ridge and Center Road, in Hinckley, Ohio. The exact location is 1634 Center Road. Over the years, the house has had fourteen different owners, and its rooms were often rented by traveling salesmen. The house had many names over the years, such as the Merchant House, the Hinckley Library and, currently, the Hinckley Historical Society. This house also has many reports of ghosts inhabiting its hallways, stairs and basement. As I walk around and through the house, I wonder if these ghosts are watching me. I peer through the window where a ghost effectively named the Lady in Blue is reported to haunt the house. Is she staring back at me? The Lady in Blue is believed to be the spirit of Rebecca Wilcox, who lived on the property with her father, Dr. Orlando Wilcox, whose ghost is also known to frequent this location. Before we dive into the ghostly phenomena, let's learn a little more about the house and its inhabitants.

Dr. Orlando Wilcox (1809–1894) came to Hinkley in 1831 and was one of the town's original settlers. Shortly after arriving in what would become Hinckley, he built a log cabin on the corner of what are now Center and Ridge Roads. Dr. Wilcox lived with his wife, Lucy Wilcox (1809–1886), and six children; the most notable include Nelson Wilcox (1830–1912), Rebecca Wilcox (1837–1896), Orlando Wilcox Jr. (1851–1932) and Lucy Wilcox (1844–1920). The property and log cabin were eventually purchased in 1846 by Mary and Samuel Raymond, who demolished the cabin and built their dream home. The house would become known as the Merchant

Hinckley Historical Society. *Katrina Massullo.*

House and would change hands several times over the course of 115 years. It was built on a foundation of sandstone blocks, which were taken from the quarry behind the Maple Hill Cemetery in Hinckley, and most of its original features remain. To this day, it has the original staircase and banister leading up the stairs.

One of the most notable families that occupied the house was the Stouffers, of frozen food fame. If you've ever heated up a frozen meal in your microwave, you can thank (or curse) Vernon Stouffer for that experience. In 1954, Stouffer's Frozen Food Company changed the way Americans ate by creating reasonably priced home-style frozen foods. The Stouffer Corporation is internationally known; however, its roots are actually in Medina County. In 1905, Abraham Stouffer and his son James Stouffer opened the Medina County Creamery Company in Medina, Ohio. In 1920, Abraham Stouffer sold the Medina County Creamery Company and, with those profits, decided to get into the restaurant business. The family had decided to freeze their most popular meals and sell them to families to heat up in their ovens at their leisure. The restaurant business was good for the Stouffers, and eventually the reins were handed over to Vernon Stouffer, who would become a pioneer in the frozen food and microwaveable foods industry, turning the family business into household name. Vernon Stouffer is also known locally as the owner of the Major League baseball team the Cleveland Indians from 1966 to 1972, a period that, according to the Encyclopedia of Cleveland, Vernon described as "the longest five years of his life." Those of us who are Cleveland sports fans know the underlying meaning of this statement. Vernon once recalled his time in the Merchant House in Hinckley, stating that he recovered from measles in one of its rooms when his maternal grandparents lived there.

In the 1960s, the Standard Oil of Ohio (SOHIO) company purchased the property, with plans to demolish the Merchant House and build a gas station. These plans met some resistance from local government and residents. Due to refusal from surrounding residents to sell their properties and drainage issues, SOHIO deemed the property unusable, and the house was abandoned. The once glorious and inviting Merchant House was boarded up and considered unsafe. With every year that passed, it continued to deteriorate due to the harsh Ohio winters, until a grassroots organization called the Friends of Hinckley Library convinced SOHIO to lease them the land in 1973 with the plan to renovate the house and turn it into a library. The Hinckley Library was officially opened in 1975.

It was during the renovations in 1973 that the first ghostly sighting occurred. Elaine Vanderschrier, a volunteer on the restoration project and later a library employee, was stopped at the red light on the corner of Center and Ridge Roads. In *Haunted Ohio III*, Elaine Vanderschrier states, "I happened to glance at a window that was in the hallway and noticed a light was burning. I could see a young woman sitting on the stairs. She wore a blue dress and had her elbows on her knees and her chin in her hands." The young woman also was noted to have a dress with a high neckline and an old-fashioned hairstyle. Elaine thought that it was odd for a young woman to be alone, sitting on the staircase, in old-fashioned clothing, in a house that was under construction; however, she assumed it was one of the workers or perhaps a worker's daughter staying late with her dad while he worked on completing renovations to the house. The next day, Elaine checked the work log and discovered that nobody was in the building that evening. This was the first of many reported sightings of the Lady in Blue.

When the library officially opened in 1975, ghostly sightings and poltergeist activity were as common as checking out a book. Footsteps on empty staircases, sensed presences while someone was alone in the library and books falling off shelves for no apparent reason were common occurrences. The books that jumped off the shelves were not random; they often involved paranormal topics, such as ghosts or extrasensory perception

The window where the Lady in Blue was first witnessed, Hinckley Historical Society.
Brandon Massullo.

(ESP), or they had "devil" in the title. People driving by the library at night would witness spirits walking (or floating) with a light or candle in the library and around the property. A local technician installing a ventilation fan in the basement made the mistake of staying well past dark. Alone in the library, he started to feel a presence and believed someone had walked into the building to speak with him. He figured it was staff checking up on him and went about his business. Lifting his head from his work, he noticed someone sitting on the basement steps. As he walked over to speak with the person, they vanished without a trace. The technician ran from the library, leaving his tools behind.

One day, Diane Dermody, the library's branch manager, was alone in the library in the early morning hours. Sitting in her office on the second floor, she was suddenly overwhelmed with a sense of fear, felt a presence and believed that she was not alone in the library. Diane attempted to walk down the staircase; however, she later wrote, "I couldn't get down the stairs because something was blocking them." She then heard a knock at the door, looked out the window and, to her surprise, saw no car or person. A few minutes later, she heard another mysterious knock.

The main staircase seems to be a hot spot for the ghosts of Hinckley Library. The bottom of the staircase is where Elaine first witnessed the Lady

The bottom of the basement steps of the Hinckley Historical Society, where an apparition was witnessed by a technician. *Brandon Massullo.*

Staircase at the Hinckley Historical Society. *Brandon Massullo.*

in Blue. The top of the staircase is where Diane Dermody was mysteriously blocked or held by an invisible force. Peering through the banister of this very staircase, a ghostly shadow man wearing a top hat has been witnessed by staff. The library staff member who witnessed the apparition spoke to a journalist at the *Akron Beacon Journal* on the condition of anonymity, reporting, "He was sitting on the stairs.…I saw him turn and look at me. I really couldn't make out the figure. I knew right away it wasn't a real person." This man is believed to be Dr. Orlando Wilcox, who once resided in a log cabin on the property. Dr. Wilcox was a short man who carried a cane, often wore a top hat and was always neatly dressed. He is described in the *History of Hinckley* as a "walking encyclopedia" and "sage" of the community; he practiced medicine, taught Sunday school and was a town clerk. It was said that whether he was farming, teaching or tending to the sick, he always wore his top hat. Because of his love of education, books and top hats, the staff believe this ghostly man with the hat must be Dr. Wilcox.

The Lady in Blue who is reported to haunt the house is suspected to be Rebecca Wilcox, the daughter of Dr. Wilcox. Rebecca and her stunning blue dress have been seen in the upstairs corridor and in the basement. Rebecca Wilcox was a well-known seamstress in her day, and according to

The bottom of the staircase at Hinckley Historical Society where the Lady in Blue and the shadow figure wearing a top hat were witnessed. *Brandon Massullo.*

A.R. Weber's *History of Hinckley*, she was "handsome in form and features and beautiful in character, artistic in her taste and skilled with her needle. Anything that came from her hand in the dress line was regarded as the best." While tilling a garden in the front of the library, staff unearthed a pair of embroidery scissors, which they believed once belonged to Rebecca.

In the book *Haunting Experiences*, Michelle Bellanger, a native of Hinckley, recalls her encounter with the Lady in Blue:

> *She had dark hair, lots of it, and it was all piled up on top of her head.... The dress was a very pale blue, almost white, and it had all these little blue flowers on it. There were about a million tiny buttons that ran up the back to a high, delicately laced collar.*

Belanger describes the Lady in Blue as being "pretty but sad." The encounter occurred in a room on the second floor; however, Belanger is not specific regarding the exact room—which is understandable, as she was four when she witnessed the Lady in Blue.

A psychic in the area was asked to visit the library on June 4, 1998. During her walkthrough of the library, she sensed the spirit of Rebecca Wilcox (known to most as Becca), as well as the negative energy of an evil male spirit. This evil spirit was described as "having deeply sunken eyes" and a "hawk-like nose." She believed this lonesome man had died in the second-floor room in the front of the house. This man was believed to have physically abused Becca; the psychic had visions of Becca covered in scars, as if she had been whipped or caned. The psychic was unable to verify who this evil male spirit was; however, she believed it to be either a lover or family member who had impregnated Becca. Due to this being scandalous at the time, the psychic had a vision of Becca being killed in her room on the second floor. The psychic believed that the murder was very gruesome, as Becca was struck in the back of the head with an axe. The psychic's impressions are documented in a Channel 5 News story as well as personal correspondence in the Medina Library reference records. Hinckley library staff handed the embroidery scissors they believed were Becca's to the psychic, and she immediately became faint. She verified the scissors indeed belonged to Becca. The psychic continued that, when she grabbed the scissors, she had a vision of Becca on her knees defending herself from attacks with these very scissors by the evil man. He grabbed the scissors from Becca and threw them out the window, only for them to be found over one hundred years later by library staff. Throughout her visit to the library, the psychic noted on several occasions visions of roses associated with Becca; however, she was unsure of their meaning. Upon leaving the library, the psychic visited the grave of Rebecca Wilcox in Maple Cemetery. While at Rebecca's grave, the psychic reported that there were roses carved on the headstone, and she claimed to hear a disembodied voice state:

> *I lie here beneath this grave, an axe within my head, the tombstone above me now, the roses there instead. They were supposed to crown my head.*

While I was combing through newspaper articles, personal correspondence and internet stories regarding the haunting of Hinckley Library, things got really muddy and confusing. The identity of the ghosts often change. Some accounts suggest that Rebecca died as a child. Others report that the Lady in Blue is not Dr. Wilcox's daughter but rather his sister or granddaughter. Some accounts suggest that the ghost in the top hat was not Dr. Wilcox but his son Nelson Wilcox. Nelson is often credited with being an early settler and physician; however, he was neither. To make things more confusing, Dr. Orlando Wilcox's third son was also named Orlando Wilcox. What I believe is clear is that none of the Wilcoxes ever lived in the house that was built in 1845 but rather a log cabin on the property that was demolished. According to historical accounts, the log cabin the Wilcoxes resided in stood on the southeast corner of the village of Hinckley on twenty-five to thirty acres. The exact location of the cabin is not clear.

Is Rebecca Wilcox the Lady in Blue? Looking at the history of the house, this would seem unlikely. Rebecca never lived or died in the house; therefore, her room is not on the second floor. Nor was she murdered there. Rebecca Wilcox died on February 3, 1869, at ten in the morning at the residence of Mrs. J.B. Parish in Cleveland, Ohio. Rebecca was thirty-two years old at her death, and according to *The History of Hinckley*, "Her untimely death in youth was mourned by the entire township for none knew her but to love her." At the time of her death, George and Elizabeth Waite lived in the house on the corner of Center and Ridge Roads. Since Rebecca never lived in or died in the house, the idea that her embroidery scissors were tossed out the window while she was being attacked is unlikely as well. Numerous families and renters resided in the house, and embroidery was not that uncommon in the late 1800s and early 1900s, meaning those scissors could have belonged to any number of people. Perhaps they are Vernon Stouffer's grandmother's scissors. I also visited the grave of Rebecca Wilcox and have

Rebecca Wilcox's grave, Maple Hill Cemetery. *Brandon Massullo.*

included a picture. There are no roses etched on the monument, as the psychic proclaimed.

I recently visited the Hinckley Historical Society on a warm and sunny April afternoon. I toured the house with Emma Schulte, who is the vice president of the Hinckley Historical Society. The house is small; however, it's briming with history. Emma knew very little about the rumors of ghosts in the house; however, she noted that staff used to place a woman's mannequin dressed in blue in the front window as a nod to the ghostly rumors. Emma has spent almost ten years volunteering at the house and has spent several hours alone in the house. When asked if she has had any ghostly occurrences or odd experiences, she replied, "Nope."

As humans, we feel inclined to solve mysteries; however, when it comes to ghostly encounters, perhaps it's best to focus on the enchanting experiences rather than trying to identify the ghosts. The Hinckley Library, now the Hinckley Historical Society, may indeed house spirits of the past; however, with so many people passing through its doors, identifying its spirits may be impossible.

CHAPTER 4

THE WOMAN IN BLACK

In 1906, the village of Medina was being terrorized. As the sun set and darkness blanketed the village, a ghost, the likes of which the village had never seen, imposed its anger on anyone foolish enough to venture out. The threat was so serious that a curfew was set to keep townspeople safe from the negative entity. According to the *Medina Gazette*:

> *The Woman in Black, that awesome specter, haunting the hedgerows, spectrally standing like impending doom in the dark shadows, creeping like a ghoul from one darkness to another in Medina Village, has come to haunt the minds of the whole town.*

The Woman in Black had been witnessed by over twenty local residents, all of whom ran in fear. She was a horrifying and intimidating sight, leaving those who dared cross her path trembling and panicked. She was described as wearing a long raven-black dress, a black hat and a veil that covered her face. She frequented what is now the Medina Square, and speculation ran amok as the town tried to comprehend what caused the wrath of this dark phantom.

On the night of Wednesday, November 14, 1906, George Santee, Charlie Moroff and their wives were returning home from the local lodge via horse-drawn carriage. Casual conversation soon turned to fear as the group encountered the Woman in Black. The apparition was several yards in front of them, making very dramatic gestures with its arms and hands. The apparition was a fair distance away; however, the couples noted ghostly

Above: Medina Square, 1907. *Courtesy of the Medina County Historical Society.*

Right: Medina woman dressed in black from the early nineteenth century. *Courtesy of the Medina County Historical Society.*

noises that sounded very close to them. George Santee, a local painter and universally liked and respected man in Medina, jumped from the carriage and gave chase to the ghost. The negative entity, demon or soul of a restless woman who had been terrorizing the village ran away! A chase ensued, and Santee, determined to bust this ghost, tackled the Woman in Black, pinning her to the ground. In a stunning turn of events, the "Woman in Black" turned out to be a local man, dressed in women's clothing, named Otto Hatchenburg. Hatchenburg's accomplice was Harry Davenport, who was responsible for making the ghostly noises while hidden in proximity to the carriage. The terror of the Woman in Black was over, and the residents of Medina could sleep peacefully once again.

I imagine Hatchenburg being dragged away by police like every costumed villain in *Scooby Doo*, yelling, "And I would have gotten away with it, too, if it weren't for that meddling George Santee!" The story took another odd turn when Otto Hatchenburg and Harry Davenport wrote a letter to the editor of the *Medina Gazette* in which they attempted to clear a few things up regarding the events of November 19. According to Hatchenburg and Davenport, they were out that night to scare a few of their friends who were returning from a party. They mistook Santee, Moroff and their wives for their friends and meant no harm to them. The men went on to state that this was the only occasion that they dressed as the Woman in Black and were not responsible for the other sightings. Do you believe the young men? Does the Woman in Black still haunt the Medina Square?

CHAPTER 5
MAIN STREET CAFÉ

If you are looking to eat, drink and gather, then the place for you is 17 Public Square on the west side of Medina Square. This restaurant is as local as they come: the current owners, Ryan and Mia Rose, as well as the head chef, Ryan Kasson, all went to Medina High School. One could say they are happy to "bee" in Medina (horrible high school mascot pun). The building where the restaurant is situated has a long and storied past. While this location has had many different owners, it has primarily housed clothing stores, grocery stores and an office supply wholesaler. In 1987, Gary Quesada bought High's Office Supply Company and renovated the space into the Main Street Café, which served patrons from 1987 to 2018. Turning the building into a restaurant required significant renovations, which were suspected to have angered the building's ghostly inhabitants. In 1988, Quesada became the first to openly discuss the ghostly occurrences when staff of the café were frequently harassed by a menacing figure. Fed up with poltergeist activity, the presence of a shadow man and ghostly attacks on employees, Quesada reached out to a local psychic for help in 2003.

The ghostly notoriety of the Main Street Café was amplified due in large part to articles in 2003 and 2004 in the *Medina Gazette* in which "Psychic Sonja" (Sonya Horstman) claimed that the ghost of a Medina farmer named Daniel, from the 1830s, haunted the restaurant due to being improperly buried on the site. These newspaper articles chronicled the spiritual tug-of-war between the ghost farmer and Psychic Sonja for the very soul of the building. According to Sonya Horstman (Psychic Sonja), the ghost that

17 Public Square restaurant, formerly Main Street Café. *Katrina Massullo.*

terrorized the restaurant was a farmer named Daniel who moved to Medina from Cleveland against his parents' wishes and ultimately died during a "wintertime cholera epidemic." Psychic Sonja claimed that because of the masses of dead due to the epidemic, the bodies began to pile up, as the ground was too frozen to dig. She believed Daniel was never properly buried due to some unfortunate mistake that led to his bones being placed in the wall just inside the back door of the building adjacent to the café, which in 2004 was Leaf and Bean Café (currently House of Hunan). She claims that during renovations, bones and an urn were discovered and thrown in the garbage, which angered the spirit. According to the newspaper article from 2004, the Main Street Café shares a brick wall with what was once Branch and Longacre Furniture and Funeral Services (currently House of Hunan). Furniture stores and cabinetmakers often performed funeral and undertaking services, since they had the tools and staff to make coffins. According to Psychic Sonja, "Next door was a cabinet maker and during the cholera epidemic he made coffins." It is implied that Branch and Longacre Furniture and Funeral Services was responsible for misplacing the remains of Daniel, leading to his restless spirit haunting the building.

The most frequent sightings in the restaurant involve ghostly shadows going up and down the stairs to the basement dining room. Staff often reported a "sense of a presence" while alone in the basement. A waitress gives an account of setting up a dinner party in the basement, being careful to meticulously arrange the tablecloth, set the silverware precisely in its proper place and light the candles to create an ambiance for the guests. She went back up the steps to further prepare for the gathering, only to return minutes later and find the table in disarray.

While trying to locate the cause of noisy pipes in the basement, a local plumber was shocked and terrified when, out of nowhere, the faucet turned on by itself and began to spray hot water on full blast. Staff would often report faucets turning on by themselves in the late hours. They described unexplained rushes of wind across their faces, as if a ghost had run by. On Halloween night in 2004, the angry spirt of Daniel reportedly attacked a dishwasher named Rick Slayer. At the beginning of his shift on Halloween night, Slayer said, his silver military compass, which he wore around his neck, broke and fell into the sink without being touched. Later in his shift, Slayer was changing a lightbulb when it exploded. Exploding lightbulbs are common at the restaurant and believed to be a favorite trick of Daniel's. Reaching into the socket to remove the bulb's base, Slayer cut his thumb

Staircase to basement dining area where ghostly figures have been witnessed, 17 Public Square *Katrina Massullo.*

Basement dining area, 17 Public Square. *Katrina Massullo.*

and began to bleed. After cutting his thumb, Slayer told his coworkers that he was going to send the ghost "back to hell." Later that evening, Slayer fell down the basement stairs and significantly injured his neck and shoulder. Did he fall, or was he pushed by the angry spirit who haunts this café?

I met with Ryan and Mia Rose, who are the current owners of 17 Public Square (formerly Main Street Café), to discuss the haunted history of the building. Mia was essentially raised in the restaurant, as her father was Gary Quesada, who owned and operated the Main Street Café. The Roses bought the restaurant three years ago and completely renovated the space. They tore up the floor, removed most of the Victorian décor and made numerous other updates to the restaurant. Ghost enthusiasts often believe that renovations or changes in the environment anger spirits, so I asked about the activity in the restaurant since they renovated. According to Ryan, "No activity since we opened." Mia stated that she has been in the restaurant "day and night" and has never experienced any ghostly phenomena. Mia thinks that if a ghost or spirit was in the restaurant, perhaps it was attached to an object—or even a staff member—that is no longer part of the restaurant. What about the ghost farmer who reportedly terrorized the staff? Mia looked shocked, stating, "I don't remember any of that happening." Both can recall stories from previous staff members; however, the phenomena were never malicious and mostly playful, such as objects moving or just disappearing altogether. The spirit that previous staff most often reported was that of a playful little girl. Ryan does recall an encounter that was reported to him several years ago by a repairman. According to Ryan, the repairman was walking down the back steps to the lower-level kitchen and felt a presence next to his shoulder. As he turned around to investigate, he witnessed a full-torso apparition of a man staring at him. The apparition was described as being tall and looking like an Amish man with a top hat. Was this Daniel the ghost farmer?

The resident ghost that I hoped to find out more information on is Daniel the ghost farmer, who was reported to be a farmer in Medina in the 1830s. Unfortunately, there were probably hundreds of farmers in Medina with the name Daniel, and with no surname it would be impossible to track him down conclusively. What we do have is other information that Psychic Sonja provided that could be useful. We have a date range in which he reportedly died (1830s), a cause of death (cholera), a time of death (winter) and, most notably, a location (his bones were found in the wall between Main Street Café and House of Hunan).

According to Psychic Sonja and her paranormal investigators, Daniel died in the 1830s during a "wintertime" cholera epidemic. Cholera is a bacterial

Back staircase, 17 Public Square. An apparition of man with a hat was witnessed here. *Katrina Massullo.*

infection that is contracted through contaminated food and water. People with cholera suffer from vomiting, diarrhea and cramps, often dying within twenty-four hours due to dehydration. Cholera reached the United States in 1832, apparently arriving with European immigrants. It quickly spread from Cleveland to Cincinnati, where in 1849 it killed eight thousand people. The date of 1830 seems unlikely for Daniel's death, as cholera had not reached the United States; however, perhaps the death occurred in the late 1830s or 1840s. If this is the case, let's look at another aspect of the story, which is that Daniel died in the winter. As noted by Psychic Sonja, Daniel's bones were not buried immediately after his death due to the rising numbers of dead from the wintertime epidemic piling up, as the ground was too frozen to dig. This part of the story also seems unlikely, as cholera deaths typically occurred in the spring, summer and fall—the cold Ohio winters killed the cholera-causing bacteria—which makes it unlikely, though not impossible, that the dead were piling up in the winter.

Let's say some ethereal wires got crossed and Daniel did not die of cholera; perhaps he died of another illness over the winter. We can further speculate that Daniel's body was, in fact, piled up waiting to be buried and somehow forgotten (I could not find any records about bones being found; however, this doesn't mean they weren't). Even if we assume this to be true and open up the range of the dates of his alleged death from 1830 to 1850, then we must also take into account the location where his bones were allegedly recovered. The building where 17 Public Square and House of Hunan currently sit was actually a grocery store called J.H. Albro and Son Grocery from 1836 to 1854; therefore, I'm not sure why they would have bodies or bones pilling up. Longacre and Branch Furniture and Funeral Services did not move into the building till 1894, which would have been sixty-four years after Daniel's alleged death. The notion that furniture makers and funeral service providers shared the wall with the future site of the Main Street Café in the 1830s, '40s or '50s is not true. Also of note is that the Medina Square suffered two disastrous fires, which completely destroyed the entire business district in 1848 and again in 1870. The fire of 1870 destroyed the Bostwick and Albro buildings, which is where the current 17 Public Square and adjacent businesses stand. The buildings literally burned to the ground and had to be rebuilt. It's hard to imagine that after two fires and numerous building renovations over two hundred years that these bones would just magically lie untouched from 1830 till 2004.

As we are finding, when researching the stories behind the hauntings of Medina County, it is very difficult to identify the exact ghostly inhabitants, and one would be better suited to simply focus on the phenomena. While it seems unlikely that a ghost farmer named Daniel is haunting the building, this does not negate the paranormal experiences that have been reported. In fact, the building does have a spooky history to it.

What is often lost in the history of this building is that Medina's most noted spiritualist owned and operated a store in the building for a brief time, where these ghostly phenomena are noted to occur. Spiritualism is a religious movement that peaked in the late nineteenth century and is based on the belief that spirits, departed souls or ghosts can communicate with the living through mediumship. Spiritualists often attend and hold séances in the hopes of opening up lines of communication with deceased loved ones. The noted spiritualist I'm referring to is Judge Albert Munson, who owned and ran a hardware store from 1886 to 1894, ultimately selling it to Fred Branch, who opened up Branch Furniture and Undertaker, which would become Branch and Longacre Furniture and Funeral Services (this would be the current House of Hunan, right next to Main Street Café). Albert Munson was a well-respected probate judge in Medina, served in the Ohio House of Representatives, was a close friend of President William McKinley and was the director of Ohio's Farmer Insurance (currently Westfield Insurance). President McKinley was so grateful for Munson's help during his presidential campaign that he offered him any position in his cabinet. Munson simply chose to be a postmaster in Medina, a role in which he served for six years. According to the *Medina County District Library Genealogy Blog*:

> *Munson believed he had a psychic link to McKinley and was convinced that the President would not live out his second term. Visiting McKinley in Canton, Munson urged the president to surround himself with guards, but McKinley replied, "Who would kill me?" Munson left, believing it would be the last time he saw his friend. And it was. McKinley was assassinated on 6 September 1901.*

Due to Munson's belief in spiritualism, he frequented local séances, and while I couldn't find any documents proving that he hosted séances at his hardware store, I suppose it wouldn't be unheard of, considering he hosted séances at his home. As a matter of fact, Munson held a séance in his home after the assignation of McKinley, hoping to communicate with his late friend and president. According to reports, the spirit of William McKinley did appear and thanked Munson for his help during the 1885 presidential campaign.

Albert Munson and the Spirit Children. *Courtesy of the Medina County Historical Society.*

In his obituary, family members noted that Munson believed "death was only an incident in a journey to other scenes." Perhaps the ghostly figures or haunt-type phenomena at the former Main Street Café were remnants of spirits who crossed over during séances; perhaps it's Judge Munson, waiting in the ether of the universe to journey to other dimensions; or could it be President William McKinley's consciousness etched into the environment, appearing only to those who are sensitive enough to detect it. While the question of who haunts the restaurant is unanswered, this should not detract from the legitimacy of the ghostly encounters reported.

It seems that the ghostly inhabitants of Main Street Café either retired or simply left once the establishment was renovated into 17 Public Square. Ryan is not a skeptic; "I'm actually a ghost guy," he says, noting that his mother was very much into the paranormal. At the request of his mother, they actually had a spiritual medium come in prior to opening 17 Public Square to check things out. According to Ryan, the medium stated, "There's nothing here." I'm not a psychic medium, but I definitely believe there is something out of this world at 17 Public Square—the food! I love their French fries and Mediterranean veggie sandwich.

CHAPTER 6

COOL BEANS CAFÉ

A s you enter Cool Beans Café at 103 West Liberty Street, your eyes are immediately drawn to the left, where an article from the *Medina Post* is displayed: "Ghosthunters Search for Spirits at Cool Beans." The article describes how three spiritual mediums and a paranormal investigation team were called to Cool Beans Café due to several paranormal concerns. According to the article, staff felt as if they were being watched in the basement, and one employee reported being pushed down the basement steps. While investigating the location, the team reportedly identified eight spirits, the most forceful of those spirits being a woman named Sandra who died in 1847. I spoke with the current owner, Laura Cavey, who has owned and operated Cool Beans Café for the past eleven years. She admits that the basement is "really creepy" and avoids it all costs. Laura stated, "I'm not a ghostly person," and she isn't sure what to make of the phenomena she and her staff have experienced. She recounts an evening when she was talking to her business partner over the phone and the conversation switched to the ghosts in the café. Laura admits to making some jokes and being dismissive of the "ghosts," only to enter the café the next day to find that most of the lightbulbs were mysteriously burnt out. Bizarre electrical issues (cash registers operating by themselves), shadow figures, lights turning on and off and lightbulbs burning out are common phenomena reported by staff. Reports by recent staff and local psychics are of at least two older male ghosts, a spirit of a child and an older female ghost.

Cool Beans Café, 2021. *Brandon Massullo.*

Most basements are creepy, and basements built in the late 1800s are even creepier, but the basement at Cool Beans Café is the kind of creepy that creates nightmares. It's the kind of creepy that horror movies and books are based on. As a matter of fact, the basement houses a well that is reminiscent of the well in the 2002 movie *The Ring*, which tells the story of the ghost of a female child who died in a well. Along with the well from *The Ring*, the basement also has a bathroom that is eerily similar to the one in the 2004 movie *Saw*. Surprisingly enough, paranormal phenomena are tied to both of these areas in the basement. The two male ghosts and the ghost of the young girl are believed to only inhabit the basement. More specifically, they are reported to be drawn to the area around the bricked-up well. The origins of the well are not really known, as the location of Cool Beans Café is the spot where the first building was constructed on the square in 1818. Actually, it wasn't a building but a two-story log structure, and it was built before the square even existed. The log structure was unofficially called the Hickox and Badger Tavern after its owners, Austin Badger (1793–1883) and Alonzo Hickox. Badger and Hickox were friends who grew up in Genesee Valley, New York, and made the arduous journey to Wooster, Ohio, to visit with Hickox's brother in 1818. On the way to Wooster, they stopped in Medina at the residence of Mr. Ferris, who just so happened to be a sales agent for land in the Medina vicinity. Badger and Hickox would later return to Medina after visiting Wooster and settle in the area. In 1818, Austin Badger, with help from Alonzo Hickox, cleared the area that would become the Medina Square, and they built a two-story log structure on the northwest corner (where Cool Beans Café currently stands). The two-story log structure housed a courtroom on the second floor and a tavern on the ground floor. Badger, who was single at the time, lived on the first floor. This tavern was an important place for the early settlers, as many meetings were held there to discuss the future and organization of Medina. One has to remember that at the time, the location that would become the square was essentially in the woods, with the nearest house being four miles away. Along with essentially creating the Medina Square and building Medina's first tavern and courthouse, Badger was also the first to own land in Montville and participated in the Great Hinckley Hunt.

The log structure was eventually torn down, and in 1847, a huge brick structure called the Empire Block was erected. The first store to occupy 103 West Liberty Street in the Empire Block was Bronson's Dry Goods, Grocery and Hardware Store. Since then, this address has housed many businesses, including physicians' offices, clothing stores, a stove shop, a shoe store, grocery stores, pharmacies and a pool hall. In 1997, the location was

Bricked-up well, Cool Beans Café, 2021. *Brandon Massullo.*

Basement bathroom, Cool Beans Café, 2021. *Brandon Massullo.*

renovated into a coffeehouse called Arabica Coffee. In 2003, the coffee shop was sold and the name changed to Cool Beans Café, which it remains today. It should also be noted that the Empire Block suffered extensive damage in the fire of 1877 and had to be rebuilt.

The well in the basement is strange and creepy, however. Laura refuses to even set foot in the basement bathroom of Cool Beans Café. As I entered the bathroom to take pictures, she proclaimed, "Oh no, I would never do that." The light in the bathroom has been a source of mystery for Laura. She reports that when she began working at Cool Beans Café, the light did not work. She changed the bulb and hit every switch in the building, but it simply would not turn on. Since the basement bathroom is not functioning, she simply moved on to bigger and more important tasks. Several years ago, for no apparent reason, the light simply turned on—and has stayed on continuously since. According to Laura, "Bad wiring doesn't fix itself."

The ghost of the older female mentioned earlier was reported to frequent the ladies' room next to the stairs leading down to the basement. Laura says that they had a cleansing a few years ago, and the medium sensed that the female ghost had "crossed over." Since then, there have been no reports of the female spirit. While Laura is unsure of the existence of ghosts, she definitely errs on the side of caution when it comes the spirits of Cool Beans

Café. Laura states, "I say 'Hi guys!' when I arrive and 'Bye guys!' when I leave, just to be on the safe side," noting that replacing lightbulbs that burn out due to angry spirits is a costly endeavor.

I could not uncover any information regarding the origins of the ghosts of Cool Beans Café. The location and space have been occupied by so many businesses, employees, patrons and owners over the years, it would be very challenging to pin down any one point in history that could have created the story or spirit. Cool Beans Café is a great location to relax and enjoy a coffee or tea overlooking the Medina Square. Just avoid the basement.

CHAPTER 7

CORKSCREW SALOON

The best way to describe the Corkscrew Saloon is "fine dining and friendly spirits." The Corkscrew Saloon at 811 West Liberty Street in Medina, Ohio, is housed in a magnificent Victorian-style mansion that dates to the late 1800s. Built by Nelson T. Burnham (1811–1882), the original structure was located on five hundred acres. Nelson Burnham was a clockmaker, businessman and farmer who moved to Medina in 1811 with his wife, Emily Clark Burnham (1817–1891) and raised eight children. Nelson T. Burnham played a critical role in rebuilding Medina's business district after the fire of 1870. Burnham owned one of the two brick kilns in Medina that pushed out over 800,000 bricks that are still visible in the downtown Medina today. The mansion has housed many restaurants over the years, including the Homestead in the 1950s, Great Expectations in the 1970s, Penny's Poorhouse in the 1990s and, currently, the Corkscrew Saloon, since 2008.

Penny's Poorhouse was named after then-owner Penny Codarini. Codarini discussed the building's ghosts in a 1991 article in the *Medina Gazette*, reporting that she believed the spirits of four or five children haunted the location. Penny and her husband lived in the apartment above the restaurant and would often come home and find the furniture rearranged. Codarini said that she would regularly hear voices while alone in the building, and in one eerie encounter, the voice was whispering her name. Phantom footsteps also occurred in the building; Codarini would sit in the kitchen and hear sixteen distinct footsteps (the staircase has sixteen steps). Flashing lights,

Early photo of Burnham House, date unknown. *Courtesy of the Medina County Historical Society.*

music playing by itself on the jukebox and missing items were also common occurrences. A waitress once saw a white cat under a table in the restaurant. She pursued the cat, only to find that it had disappeared. Patrons have frequently reported witnessing ghostly apparitions standing in the windows or walking through the restaurant. One patron actually witnessed a full-body apparition of a woman in the kitchen.

Ryan and Brittany Marino have owned the Corkscrew Saloon since 2012; however, they both have also worked there since 2008. Brittany is extremely familiar with the restaurant—and the ghosts. As we took a seat in one of the many dining rooms at the restaurant, Brittany stated, "I 100 percent believe that ghosts are here." She disclosed many ghostly encounters experienced by staff and patrons over the years, stressing that the ghosts are "friendly" and she never felt threatened or fearful. She went on to state, "Every morning when I walk in and turn off the alarm, I greet the building as if it was a customer." It's clear that Brittany has a soft spot in her heart for the spirits that roam the Corkscrew Saloon, treating them with the same courtesy and respect as her staff and customers.

The most frequent spirit reported at the saloon is a young boy around six years old. He has been described as having blond hair and wearing a red sweater with a white turtleneck underneath. Tiffany, who has worked for eleven years at the Corkscrew Saloon, talked about an encounter that occurred several years back involving the boy. Tiffany's coworker had noticed two older women and a young boy waiting at the hostess stand by the main entrance. These women and the boy were the only patrons in the restaurant, as they'd just opened. The older women were eventually seated; however, the boy was nowhere to be found. This particular staff member was concerned, so she asked the women where the boy they arrived with had gone. The two women were confused, stating they came together and had not seen any boy while they were waiting at the hostess stand. Tiffany reports her coworker was visibly shaken, as she had never had a ghostly encounter before and saw this boy as clear as day. Brittany believes this young spirit is very timid, as he is seen often peering around corners and heard running up and down the stairs when Brittany is alone in the restaurant.

Before 2008, the upstairs portion of the restaurant was an apartment where the previous owners had lived. If you recall, this portion of the building was reported to be the most active when Penny Codarini and her husband lived in and ran Penny's Poorhouse. The living quarters no longer exist and have been renovated to include more dining space for patrons and

Great Expectations, 1970s. *Courtesy of the Medina County Historical Society.*

Hostess stand and staircase, a hot spot of ghostly activity at the Corkscrew Saloon, 2021. *Brandon Massullo.*

offices for Ryan and Brittany. They probably had a good contractor for the renovations; however, they failed to remove the spirits. Two female ghosts are witnessed mostly on the second floor, often hanging out in Ryan's office. Patrons who are sensitive to spirits have told Brittany that these women "enjoy Ryan's company and believe in what he has done with the building and restaurant." These female spirits are very protective of Ryan. It seems that Ryan has a couple of bodyguard entities who protect him and keep him safe. I suggest you don't mess with Ryan.

The magical properties of salt are shared by many cultures and civilizations. Salt is believed to cleanse negative energies, break hexes or curses and guard against psychic attacks. Among ghost hunters, salt is often used to repel spirits, and when poured at the entrances of your house, it is believed to keep spirits from entering. I always found it odd that a substance that is present in most foods would repel ghosts. By this logic, if you are fearful of ghosts, the best place to work would be Morton Salt Company in Rittman. Seems the ghosts at the Corkscrew are not repelled by salt but actually attracted to it. Brittany reports that Ryan came into his office one morning only to find salt scattered across his desk. This has occurred several times. Brittany and another staff member were preparing a table in the upstairs dining room.

After setting things up, they left the room for only a few moments, only to find that the saltshaker was tipped over and the salt meticulously piled up a few inches away. According to Brittany, "It was the perfect little pile of salt, and not one grain was anywhere else."

It would seem that staff and owners, even those who don't necessarily believe in ghosts, treat these ghostly inhabitants as family. Ghosts and spirits are often portrayed on TV and movies as discarnate angry spirits who want to be left alone or wish to strike fear in the living, which is not the case at the Corkscrew. Brittany said something very telling during our interview: "We don't want to scare them off." Wait, what? You mean you don't want to call the Ghostbusters? To most, the idea of living and working with ghosts seems odd; however, research states that most people indicate their ghostly experiences resulted in increased happiness and confidence, and they also reported decreased depression, loneliness, fear and dread of death. The common assumption is that paranormal experiences, such as hauntings, are a cause of distress; however, it appears that this is a short-term reaction.

The only bit of information we have from this location is that the ghosts are believed to be either several children or one six-year-old boy. There have also been several reports of apparitions of two different females who

Upstairs dining room, where salt pile was found. Corkscrew Saloon, 2021. *Brandon Massullo.*

frequently haunt the second floor. Without names, dates or descriptions, it's hard to dig up anything regarding the origins of these ghostly inhabitants. As stated above, the Burnhams had eight children; however, they did not live in the house that would become the Corkscrew Saloon. The Burnhams actually lived in another house on the property, as the brick mansion that would become known as the Burnham House was not completed until 1881. However, of the Burnhams' eight children, all of them survived into adulthood except Arthur Nelson (1847–49), who died at age two. Nelson died just prior to the Burnhams finishing the mansion on West Liberty in 1881. Josephine Burnham (1851–77) was in born in and died at a house on the property that the family lived in prior to the completion of the Burnham House in 1881. The exact location of that residence on the property is unknown. According to Josephine's obituary, she was ill with consumption for an extended period of time. She died "peacefully and happily in the arms of her father" in the house where she was raised. Josephine was twenty-five at the time of her death.

With the help of Lisa Rienerth of the Medina County Library, we were able to research the Burnham House quite thoroughly. The house was in the Burnham family till 1893, when it was purchased by Eleanor Hendrickson, who lived mostly in Washington, D.C., where her husband was a professor. Eleanor may have rented or leased the house, as records indicate that Charles Pratt and his family lived there in the late 1890s. Cora Carlton and her husband bought the house in 1910; however, they soon sold it to John Lampson in 1912. Mr. Lampson and his wife, Carrie, lived at the house until Mr. Lampson's death in 1915. The house was eventually sold in 1917 to J.M. and Martha Shive, who lived in half of the house and rented the other half out. Herman Arnosk bought the house in 1941 and eventually renovated it to include a tavern on the lower floor, which would become known as the Homestead Tavern. The house would change hands several times in the next forty years, with some tavern managers living in the upstairs apartment. In 1981, Robert and Carol Frey bought the house and tavern and changed the name to Great Expectations. While owning and running the tavern, the Freys lived in the upstairs apartment. The Codarinis purchased the house and restaurant in 1986 and changed the name to Penny's Poorhouse. They lived in the house and ran the restaurant till 2007, when it was purchased by Ginny Vargo, Ryan Marino and Steven Charnigo. This group of investors would change the restaurant's name to the Corkscrew Saloon.

Since its construction in 1881, the Burnham House has housed many individuals. Of those individuals who lived in the house, only Mr. Nelson

Burnham (the original owner), Mr. John Lampson (a later owner) and two of Mr. Lampson's grandchildren (they were both stillborn) died in the house. We were unable to find any significant traumas, accidents or deaths associated with the house.

In my opinion, the Corkscrew is the most genuine and interesting haunted location in Medina County. The ghostly encounters have been consistent over time and experienced by multiple individuals. Those who report paranormal encounters are longtime staff, frequent patrons and even first-time customers just passing through town. Penny Codarini and her husband's experiences in the 1990s are very similar to those of staff today. As a matter of fact, Penny reported often hearing a disembodied voice whispering her name, which is a very intense experience indicating some type of intelligent ghost able to interact with and learn from the environment. When I talked with longtime Corkscrew staff member Tiffany, she reported hearing this disembodied voice as well. According to Tiffany, she was preparing to open the restaurant, and aside from one other staff member, she was alone in the building. She was at the hostess stand near the main entrance, and she heard a man's voice say, "Tiffany." The voice sounded as if it came from the top of the staircase. She yelled back, "What?" There was no response, and she could see nobody at the top of the stairs. Not only was this voice unfamiliar, but she also found it strange that it called out for "Tiffany," as all her friends, family and coworkers call her "Tiff." It was also odd because the only other person in the building was in kitchen. She rushed to the kitchen to double check that he was still there, and sure enough, he was.

I absolutely love this place, and I especially love that staff are more interested in and enchanted by the paranormal phenomena than frightened of it. Staff love the ghosts at the Corkscrew Saloon, and it seems that the ghosts love them as well. So stop by the Corkscrew Saloon for lunch or dinner, where you are guaranteed to experience great food, passionate staff and friendly ghosts. Oh, and keep an eye on your salt.

CHAPTER 8

MEDINA STEAK AND SEAFOOD COMPANY

W hen I first began researching haunted locations in Medina County, I was told that the former Medina Steak and Seafood Company restaurant was the most haunted. I was enamored of the ghost stories told to me by friends and neighbors about this location. While the specifics varied, this restaurant was believed to be haunted by a friendly female ghost and an angry man who died on the second floor. Before we get into the haunted happenings at what is now Sérénité Restaurant, let's take a moment to look at the history of 538 West Liberty Street.

Mr. H.G. Blake is credited with building the first structure at 538 West Liberty Street in 1858. The purpose of the original structure is debated to this day; however, some suggest it was a stagecoach stop. H.G. Blake (1818–1876) settled in the village of Medina in 1836 at the age of seventeen. During his lifetime, Blake studied law, was elected to the U.S. House of Representatives and U.S. Congress, was a colonel in the Civil War, was a close personal friend of Abraham Lincoln, opened the first bank in Medina (Phoenix Bank), was the first editor of the *Medina Gazette* and served as mayor of Medina. Blake was in opposition of slavery, and his residence on East Washington and Jefferson Streets was an important stop on the Underground Railroad. The building at 538 West Liberty Street is also rumored to have been a stop on the Underground Railroad. Blake was a businessman who owned several properties in Medina; therefore, he most likely never lived in the West Liberty building.

In 1873, Blake sold the property for $500 to Dr. J. Palmer, who built a small hotel called the Palmer House Hotel. The Palmer House Hotel changed owners many times until, in 1884, it was sold to John Gluntz, who changed the name to the Germania House Hotel. Gluntz is noted for building the iconic veranda on the second floor that remains today. Julia and Andrew G. Miller bought the Germania House Hotel and changed the name to the Miller House Hotel in 1900. There were numerous renovations and owners over the next forty-five years; however, the Miller House Hotel name remained. In 1920, a general store opened on the lower level, and in 1925, a restaurant opened next to the general store. By 1945, the hotel was no longer in business, and the rooms became apartments. With these changes, the name was no longer accurate and was changed to the Medina Steak House. In 1984, Dale Kovalchik purchased the property, and again it was renamed: Medina Steakhouse and Saloon. In 1994, Ken Collins purchased the building, and it became the Medina Steak and Seafood Company. Mr. Collins continues to own the property, which is currently leased by Sérénité Restaurant and Culinary Institute. Sérénité is a fantastic addition to Medina County, as it's not only a great restaurant but also works in conjunction with the Recovery Center of Medina County to provide training in the restaurant business as well as addiction recovery treatment. Sérénité provides culinary training over the course of an eight-month program, which helps to change

Miller House Hotel, 1909. *Courtesy of the Medina County Historical Society.*

Sérénité Restaurant and Culinary Institute, 2021. *Brandon Massullo.*

the face of recovery by providing essential on-the-job training for students while generating revenue to support the recovery center, supplementing the cost of education. Good food, great cause—and ghosts.

The restaurant is rumored to be haunted by several ghosts. The most notable is Anna of the Inn. According to a 1981 article in the *Medina Sun Sentinel*, the owner of the building at that time, Marcelle Arndt, held Ouija board sessions during which she claimed to have contacted the spirit of "Anna." Anna is believed to be one of several sisters who worked at the inn in the late 1800s when the building was either the Germania House Hotel or the Miller House Hotel. Through numerous sessions utilizing the Ouija board, she claimed that Anna died in the building in 1895 and has chosen to remain there. Anna loves the building, and during communications with psychics and Ouija board sessions, she discussed being fond of the horse-and-carriage traffic and the traditional décor and said she was always appreciative when people chose to "dine in our gracious quarters."

The ghost of Anna is believed to be responsible for saving the building from a fire in 1979. The *Medina Sentinel* reported that "according to fire officials the fire was so hot the paint bubbled and smoldered—but the walls burned only part way up, confounding the experts." The fire started in a small room on the second floor. The building did not have a sprinkler system in 1979, yet somehow, it's rumored that the fire put itself out before it spread. Anna communicated through the Ouija board, telling Marcelle that she could not bear to see the beautiful building destroyed; therefore, she took action and stopped the spread of the fire through some supernatural means. Fire is a common theme when it comes to the haunted lore of this location, as there are variations to this story in which some patrons of the restaurant claim to have seen an apparition of a ghost surrounded by flames, believed to be a young woman who had died trying to save the building from a fire. Perhaps the young ghost engulfed in flames and Anna are one and the same? Is Anna of the Inn that young woman who died in an earlier fire? Perhaps that explains her quick response to the fire in 1979. Marcelle noted that Anna is a kind ghost who provides warmth and comfort; however, she is not too happy with changes or attempts to modernize the building.

So, who is Anna of the Inn? The ghost is often associated with fire, so I thought the first place to start would be to determine if there had been any fires at 538 West Liberty Street. The only fire of record occurred on the night of Saturday, February 17, 1979. According to the *Medina Gazette*, the fire was the result of cigarette ashes burning on a chair in a room above the restaurant (at that time, the upstairs housed small apartments). The fire was contained to one room; however, part of the ceiling collapsed due to water damage suffered as crews attempted to extinguish the fire. An elderly man was in the apartment when the fire started and, after being transported to Medina Hospital, eventually died of smoke inhalation. Nobody else was injured in the fire, and there were no reports of a female child or woman being involved.

Another pertinent detail revealed during Ouija board sessions related to the ghost known as Anna of the Inn was that she died in 1895 in the building. According to the Medina County death records for 1895, a total of four Annas died that year: Ann E. Edwards (1837–95), Ann W. French (1833–95), Anna Kleimer (1835–95) and Anna Merfelt (1853–95). None of these Annas died in the city of Medina, and most of them were farmer's wives who never worked at the hotel. Also, they all died of natural causes.

To further research Anna of the Inn, I turned to local genealogist and Medina historian Lisa Rienerth, who uncovered two likely candidates. According to Lisa,

> *I looked at all the names of the past owners and one of them caught my eye. The Germania House Hotel was bought by Andrew G. Miller and his wife Julia Anna. They ran the hotel from 1900–1917. One bit of information*

states that Mrs. A.G. Miller owned, cooked, and served meals at the Miller House Hotel in 1902. Julia Anna died in 1945 and is buried in Spring Grove Cemetery. I know this "Anna" didn't die in 1895, but she did have a history with [the building].

The other Anna possibly linked with the building at the turn of the nineteenth century is Anna Tibbitts. Anna Tibbitts (1860–1947) was a cook at the Miller House Hotel in 1906, meaning she worked side by side with the other Anna, Julia Anna Miller. Tibbitts was also a cook and server for two other hotels in Medina, making her well known in the community. Along with cooking, she also traveled the county with another woman, caring for the ill. Think of Anna Tibbitts as a home health care worker traveling the area caring and cooking for many community members. Anna also ran a "tourist home" or bed-and-breakfast in her residence on North Court Street for twenty years. So we have two women named Anna who worked together during the turn of the nineteenth century at this location. While neither died in the building, it could be possible that they looked alike or the patrons lovingly called them sisters, which could give some credibility to the story of Anna of the Inn being one of three sisters who worked at the hotel.

There are reports of another ghost haunting this restaurant that is not pleasant, kind or inviting. This ghost is believed to be the restless soul of Frank Curtis(s), a handyman, who allegedly hanged himself in the upper hallway of the inn on Christmas Eve in 1922. The exact location noted was the second-floor hallway toward the rear, right by the attic steps. This restless spirit is reported to haunt the employees and guests in very mischievous ways and take every chance to scare or strike fear in the living by suddenly opening doors and turning on the TV or radio. This angry entity once harassed a cook so much that she walked out and never returned. A chef witnessed a keg of beer move by itself in the basement. In his book *Ghosthunting Ohio*, John Kachuba interviewed a waitress at what was then the Medina Steak and Seafood Company who discussed the haunted story of Frank Curtis(s) and noted that it had been verified that his grave is in Spring Grove Cemetery and his death occurred in 1922. This important piece of information was circulated among the staff and the community at large, which makes it extremely crucial and also verifiable, so I again reached out to local historian and genealogist Lisa Rienerth to dig deeper. According to Lisa,

I did check for a death record in 1922 for any one with the name of Frank Curtis(s), or anything close to it, that died in Medina County. I did not find

Stairs to the attic, rumored to be the spot Frank Curtis(s) died. *Brandon Massullo.*

a death record. However, when I searched for a death record for a Frank Curtis in Medina County without a specific date, I did find one that died in 1941. However, his death certificate states that he died of a heart attack. He is buried in Spring Grove Cemetery with his wife.

Lisa believed that she might be able to track this further if she focused on the cause of death when searching the death records. She went on to state,

I also did a thorough search through our digital newspapers and did not find any stories about a man hanging himself at the hotel, which was known as the Miller House Hotel at the time. I did search for hangings throughout the lifetime of the building and found none. This doesn't mean there wasn't one, but it did not make the newspapers, or it didn't get picked up with my search.

The story about Frank Curtis(s) bothered me because of how specific and detailed the information surrounding his death was. We have a name, occupation (handyman), method of death (suicide), location (upper hallway) and date (Christmas Eve 1922). I kept thinking there was some truth surrounding this story. Turns out there was a *Fred* Curtiss, a handyman (painter and wallpaper hanger), who died suddenly on Christmas Day in 1914. He died a mile west of the square (very close to the Miller House Hotel) in an upstairs bedroom. Fred Curtiss had eaten Christmas dinner at the house of his friend Mr. Kaatz. Soon after eating dinner, he reported that he was feeling ill and retired to a room on the second floor. A member of the Kaatz family went to check on Fred later in the evening and found him dead on the floor. The cause of death was officially noted to be heart failure associated with alcoholism. Fred Curtiss (1849–1915) was sixty-five years old when he died. When Fred died, he most likely was grieving the loss of his only son, who died two months earlier. His son was Donald *Frank* Curtiss. There could have been some speculation and elaboration from locals regarding the death of Fred that, in a way, created a narrative that he was depressed and had died by suicide, which per the official corner's report is not true. Being a well-known handyman, it's quite possible that he worked often at the Miller House Hotel. Speculation and rumors around Mr. Curtiss's death, along with the proximity of his death to the Miller House Hotel, may have created the story of a handyman named Frank Curtiss hanging himself on the second floor of the Miller House Hotel. With every retelling of a story or rumor, the details often change, and the events are often exaggerated. Perhaps this is the case.

The third ghost reported to haunt this building is simply named "M." She is believed to be the sister of Anna of the Inn and has been witnessed by cleaning staff and waitstaff walking up the main staircase. Employees have reported a presence as they leave the restaurant watching over them to ensure their safety. One waitress felt the presence of M while driving home from work. It appears that M is a type of ghostly bodyguard for those she fancies. I'm afraid there is no history that could be uncovered about M— except to note that Mrs. Julia Anna Miller, whom we discussed earlier, did not have a sister whose name began with an *M*.

When one attempts to find the "true" identity of spirits noted to haunt a location, it often ends with more questions than answers. The truth is that people who frequent the location that is now called the Sérénité Restaurant report numerous paranormal encounters. Several children eating at the restaurant are reported to have asked their parents, "Who was the older man and the lady in the funny long dress?" Are they seeing Anna of the Inn, M or Frank Curtiss? Perhaps the spirits of others who have crossed paths with this location still linger? While the identities of the spirits are unknown, what is known is that many people died at the location on 538 West Liberty Street since it was built in 1858. Those injured in accidents were often taken to the hotel to be cared for, as there was not quick and easy access to hospitals. There are many news articles about individuals dying at the hotel after being injured on the railroad tracks nearby, suffering heart attacks or even being shot. Thomas Murphy died at what was then the Germania House after being shot by Medina deputy Barton in 1898. Murphy was reported to be a vagabond or tramp who was seeking handouts from local residents. After refusing to leave town at the request of Deputy Barton, a verbal altercation took place, and Murphy was shot. He spent seven days in pretty intense pain at the Germania House before succumbing to his injury. John H. Whitman was a railroad worker who died at the Germania House in 1893. Whitman was an engineer who was fatally injured in an accident that occurred near the Harrisville Road crossing. The engine left the track and tumbled down the embankment. Whitman jumped from the train and landed on the track.

In an article in *Cleveland Magazine*, Brandon Chrostowski, who currently runs the Sérénité Restaurant, spoke about the building's ghostly inhabitants, reporting several paranormal phenomena, including lights flickering, tables moving by themselves and apparitions of a mysterious young girl playing with toys. According to Chrostowski,

> *The mayor doesn't even come around, because he's afraid of the place....
> "There's something in that damn place," he says. "And, you know, late at
> night, you feel it."*

CHAPTER 9
SPITZER HOUSE
BED AND BREAKFAST

The Spitzer House Bed and Breakfast is located at 504 West Liberty Street, a stone's throw away from the Sérénité Restaurant (formerly known as the Medina Steak and Seafood Company). The Spitzer House is an exquisite hidden gem that's draped in both history and floral wallpaper. The most charming room in the house is the parlor, which surrounds the guest with a library of books on local history and the Spitzer family. Haunt-type phenomena are reported to be a frequent occurrence at this quaint German Renaissance–style location, with reports of unexplained music, full-body apparitions, phantom footsteps, objects being rearranged, poltergeist activity, cold spots without rational explanation, slamming doors, a sensed presence while the person was alone, spirit voices, lights flickering, unexplained music and even reports of people being touched by unseen hands.

The Spitzer House was built in 1890 by General Ceilan Milo Spitzer (1849–1919). Ceilan Spitzer was born in New York and raised in Medina. The Spitzer family has a very prestigious lineage in American history. Ceilan is a descendant of Martin Van Buren, who was America's eighth president from 1837 to 1841. After graduating from Oberlin College, Spitzer bought into a general store in Seville. After two years, he sold his part of the business and opened a bank with his father, Aaron Bovee Spitzer, called the Seville Exchange Bank. Ceilan and his father did well in the banking business,

Spitzer House Bed and Breakfast, 2021. *Brandon Masssullo.*

eventually opening branches in Medina and Cleveland. Ceilan appears to have only lived in the Spitzer house for a year or so, at which point he gave his parents a lifelong lease in 1891. Ceilan moved to Toledo, where he continued to prosper, and later died in California. Descendants of the Spitzer family lived in the house for seventy years until the passing of Evalyn Spitzer Woods in 1960. Evalyn was Ceilan's niece. The house changed hands several times and was converted to a bed-and-breakfast in 1994 by Dale and Janet Rogers. It remains a bed-and-breakfast to this day and is currently owned by Delane Nagel. Each of the four guest rooms are appropriately named after members of the Spitzer family and include Anna's Room (named after Anna Collins Spitzer, 1841–1923, who was Ceilan's stepmother), Aaron's Room (named after Aaron Bovee Spitzer, 1823–1892, who was Ceilan's father and business partner), Evalyn's Room (named after Evalyn Spitzer Woods, who was Ceilan's niece) and Ceilan's Room (named, of course, after General Ceilan Milo Spitzer).

Full-body apparitions of General Spitzer, who is known to push or nudge guests, are reported in Ceilan's Room and at the top of the staircase. Disembodied voices and doors slamming are other creepy occurrences in this particular room. The ghost of a young servant girl is believed to haunt Anna's Room and the hallways. Her laughter is heard throughout

An apparition of a young servant girl has been reported at end of this hallway in the Spitzer House Bed and Breakfast, 2021. *Brandon Massullo.*

the house, and she is often seen at the end of the long hall by the stairs that lead to the kitchen.

Chris Woodyard, author of *Haunted Ohio IV*, describes an actual conversation with a ghostly woman in Anna's Room. According to Woodyard, the ghost of a "short, stout woman, in her twenties, perhaps wearing what could have been a striped skirt and waist or what the Edwardians called a 'wrapper' or housedress" appeared suddenly as Woodyard was exiting the bathroom after taking a shower. The ghostly woman had smooth hair that was parted in the middle and a heavy jaw. The ghost asked a series of questions similar to a curious child: "How old are you? Are you pregnant? Do you have any children? What are you doing here?" Woodyard described the ghost as "very nosy and completely unselfconscious." After getting her questions answered, the ghost suddenly disappeared, seeming to have lost interest.

Phantom footsteps are heard pacing back and forth throughout the hallway and staircase. A psychic visiting Evalyn's Room reported the presence of a young boy. The piano in the parlor often plays a tune by itself, and ghostly conversations between two men are commonplace in the parlor as well.

Anna's Room, where a female ghost is reported to communicate with guests. *Brandon Massullo.*

I spent a night in Anna's Room, hoping to get a chance to speak with the ghost Woodyard had written about, however noting supernatural occurred. During my stay, I had the pleasure of speaking with the bed-and-breakfast's caretaker, Hayley, who actually lives on-site. She reported that she has lived in and managed the house for the past ten years and while she has had a couple bizarre occurrences, she has never seen an apparition. She says that she has never felt uncomfortable in the house and reports an occasional sense of a presence when alone. She describes this presence as "maternal" and believes that if it is a spirit, its role is to protect and oversee those who enter the house. She also has had previous guests report ghost cats in and around the property. Hayley was gracious enough to recall one of her unusual experiences that occurred in Aaron's Room. She awoke in the early morning hours and noticed that a balloon was in the corner of the room. This was not unusual, as there had been a birthday party earlier in the evening, and it appeared a balloon had simply wandered into her room. As she was lying in bed, she noticed that the balloon began to systematically traverse the room, going from corner to corner and then stopping in the center. When the balloon would stop in the center, it would slowly move to the floor, as if the balloon string was being tugged by a child. She reports that the balloon followed this pattern for almost an hour.

The Spitzer House is a great local place, and I highly recommend spending a couple nights or, at the very least, suggesting it to family and friends visiting from out of town. As I mentioned, I did spend a night at Spitzer House Bed and Breakfast, and the only thing I experienced that was not of this world was—the breakfast. The eggs Benedict is a spiritual experience, exquisitely prepared by Hayley. Perhaps the breakfast is so good that the dead keep returning.

CHAPTER 10

THE WITCH'S BALL

Myrtle Hill Cemetery was established in 1822 and sits just north of the intersection of Columbia Road and Myrtle Hill Road. It's just over five acres and officially rests in Valley City (Liverpool Township). Legend has it that 130 years ago, a witch preyed on the residents of Liverpool Township. The witch allegedly stole pets, performed unholy rituals and cast spells on her neighbors. The townspeople raided the witch's home near Valley City and dragged her off to trial. She was convicted and sentenced to death. The residents of Valley City were said to have buried her alive (standing up) beneath a heavy granite sphere in Myrtle Hill Cemetery. It was believed that the granite sphere would ensure that the witch would never rise from the grave. This polished granite sphere become known as the Witch's Ball. Tales quickly spread that the witch's restless spirit haunts the cemetery, looking for revenge. If you want to know if the ghostly witch's spirit is present, simply touch the sphere. If it's warm, the witch is inside her grave; however, if it's cold, the witch is roaming Valley City looking for souls.

Other variations of the story are that the sphere defies physics, as it's warm in the winter and cold in the summer. It's also said that snow is unable to stick to the sphere and that leaves from nearby trees refuse to fall anywhere near the sphere. On rare occasions, a mysterious woman dressed in black is seen near the Witch's Ball. This ghostly mourner is said to be grieving and is reported to leave a single black rose near the Witch's Ball. Is this stranger a descendant of the witch? An admirer? Or perhaps the witch herself? There are other variations of this legend that state the witch was not buried alive

Witch's Ball in Myrtle Hill Cemetery. *Katrina Massullo.*

but stoned to death. According to another version, an insane woman who poisoned her family and threw them down a well is buried under the granite stone known as the Witch's Ball.

In actuality, the Witch's Ball is not a grave but rather a family headstone or memorial for the Stoskopf family. In addition to individual headstones, a family may choose to erect a memorial that serves as a focal point for the resting place of their entire family. In the case of the Stoskopf family, the polished granite sphere that has become known as the Witch's Ball stands in front of the individual headstones of George Stoskopf (1862–1949); his wife, Alma Stoskopf (1878–1943); their daughter Helen Toth (1904–1995); and Helen's husband, Joseph Toth (1899–1978). Lucille Stoskopf was interviewed in 2000 and 2003 when she was in her eighties regarding the legends behind the Witch's Ball. In a 2000 *Akron Beacon Journal* article titled "Graveyard Visitors Keep Eye on the Polished Granite Ball," Lucille stated, "I know for a fact that they weren't buried standing up….I witnessed the burial." According to Lucille, her mother-in-law (Alma Stoskopf) simply asked for a family plot marker that was unusual, and the sphere is what they came up with. There is actually another Stoskopf family plot and monument about twenty-five feet away from the Witch's Ball; however, that monument is more traditional.

What is fascinating is trying to piece together the origin story of the Witch's Ball. Of all the strange and unusual family monuments and headstones in cemeteries across Medina County, why did a story about a witch terrorizing townspeople get attached to the Stoskopf family marker at the Myrtle Hill Cemetery? As I'm finding out, there's usually a crumb of truth to folklore and haunted locations. The first crumb leads us to Martha Wise, who lived not far from Myrtle Hill Cemetery.

Martha Wise (1884–1971), born Martha Hasel, is the real "witch" of Valley City. Martha was born in the little town of Hardscrabble (which is now Valley City) in Medina County. She is an internationally known serial killer dubbed the "Poison Widow of Hardscrabble" or the "Borgia of America." At the age of twenty-two, Martha married Albert Wise, moved to his fifty-acre farm and, over the next seventeen years, had four children. Albert died mysteriously in 1923 of blood poisoning. At the time, nobody suspected Martha of the crime, as locals described her as simple, feeble-minded, slow-witted and odd—but not dangerous. While she was always a social recluse who exhibited eccentric behavior, after her husband's funeral, her eccentricity grew more concerning to her family. She became obsessed with death and never missed a funeral. She would walk twenty miles both ways to attend the funeral of someone she never knew. Her behavior at funerals also

Myrtle Cemetery. *Katrina Massullo.*

drew the attention of her community, as she would cry excessively, wail and moan over the caskets of people she had never met.

About a year after her husband's death, Martha fell in love with John Walters, a farmhand who worked adjacent to her home. Martha's mother, Sophie Hasel, her aunt Lillian (Lily) Gienke, and the Wise family frowned on the relationship, which caused great conflict. Martha's mother threatened to disown her if she continued to be seen with John Walters. Martha reluctantly ended the relationship and showed up to the family's Thanksgiving dinner in 1924 alone, angry and with arsenic (poison). After dinner, Martha's mother and several family members became ill. Most of the family recovered; however, Sophie Hasel, Martha's mother, died on December 13, 1924. Again, nobody suspected Martha, and after a grieving period, the family again met for a holiday dinner on New Year's Eve at the Gienke household. Prior to dinner, Martha poured arsenic into the water buckets and instructed her children to never drink the water at the Gienke house. Soon after dinner, the entire Gienke family became ill with severe stomach pains and were eventually hospitalized. Martha would continue to visit the Gienkes in the hospital, often poisoning their water or offering them poisoned fruit that she brought with her. Physicians were baffled as to why the Gienkes were not responding to treatment and even getting sicker while in the hospital. Martha's aunt, Lily Gienke, and uncle, Fred Gienke, would eventually die. In total, she had poisoned seventeen family members; three of them died, two would be partially paralyzed and twelve became severely ill. Exactly how Martha became the primary suspect is unclear. I like the story that the local sheriff was investigating another case and, while looking through a local drugstore's records, noticed that Martha had purchased large quantities of arsenic. The sheriff's suspicions eventually resulted in an autopsy, which revealed arsenic in the stomach of Lily Gienke. During questioning, according to a *Toledo Bee* article in 1930, Martha confessed to the poisonings, stating, "The devil put me up to it."

Martha's true motives for the killings have always been unclear. During the trial, Martha claimed that it was her fascination with funerals; since there weren't enough funerals in the community, she felt compelled to create more by killing. She also claimed that she was instructed to kill by the devil and other voices. Toward the end of the trial, she claimed that her lover, John Walters, convinced her to kill her family so they could be together. In a twist, John Walters denied that he even had a romantic relationship with Martha, stating he only visited her on occasion, and that was due to pity. No matter the motive, Martha was convicted of first-degree murder and sentenced to life in prison.

DEATH HER ONLY THRILL

. . . .

Widow Poisons Own Mother, Uncle, Aunt and Decimates Families With Fifteen 'Water Bucket' Murders

MEDINA, Ohio, March 28.—Mrs. Martha Wise, 43-year-old Hardscrabble widow liked to go to funerals.
    People didn't die often enough in Hardscrabble to satisfy Widow Wise's morbid appetite.
So Widow Wise made her own funerals.
    She killed her mother, her aunt and her uncle, and almost wiped out their families.
    Widow Wise walked miles to attend a funeral. She had not missed a funeral in 20 years in her home town. A week ago she went to Cleveland over almost impassable roads to attend the funeral of a distant relative.
    Today the State of Ohio demands that Widow Wise die for causing funerals she liked to attend.

Martha Wise headline, 1925. *Courtesy of the Los Angles Record.*

Martha Wise's trial made headlines across the country. The facts of the case became blurred as each journalist exaggerated certain details. A lonely woman with cognitive deficits and mental illness soon morphed into an evil woman fascinated with witchcraft and devil worshipping. The facts of the case slowly turned into fiction. A story in the 1942 edition of the *American Weekly* titled "The Devil in Hardscrabble Alley" portrayed the events that occurred in Hardscrabble as being related to witchcraft, black magic and the devil:

> *Never had Hardscrabble Valley known such stark, unreasoning terror. The God-fearing farmers, who scratched a frugal living from its grudging, stony soil, pulled up their horses when they met on the almost deserted roads. "Where will it strike next?" they asked, looking behind them as they spoke. "Who will be next to go?" Their frightened wives, gathering at the bedside of a sick neighbor, for only a major catastrophe could get them to stir far from their own doorsteps, asked the same thing.*
>
> *Why had the Evil One selected this remote county in northern Ohio for his unholy attention? Why had he picked their homes and areas to blast with fire and brimstone, themselves and their cattle with mysterious, agonizing death? What had they done to deserve this terrible affliction that was being visited upon them?…A wave of mass hysteria swept the Valley. Where would the Devil strike next? Who would be next to go? What—oh, what have we done to deserve all this?*

Let's get back to the connections between Martha Wise and the Witch's Ball in Myrtle Hill Cemetery. Martha actually lived less than a mile from Myrtle Hill Cemetery on Grafton Road. Due to her fascination with funerals, she must have attended numerous ones at Myrtle Hill Cemetery, which could explain some connection. OK, so she was a murderer and lived near the cemetery; that still doesn't explain the accusations of witchcraft. There are plenty of murderers who aren't associated with witchcraft, so why is Martha Wise?

First, let's look at common stereotypes and misconceptions about witches that have been portrayed in books, movies, TV and society for the past several hundred years. Spells, hexes and curses by witches were often blamed for troubles with livestock, unknown disease and sudden deaths. It was believed that witches had pacts with the devil, were followers of Satan, practiced black magic, performed unholy rituals in the woods at night and could change into animal forms. Witches were generally seen as evil women who took instruction from Satan himself. During the trial of Martha Wise, several members of Hardscrabble (Valley City) talked at length of her eccentric behaviors. Along with her fascination with death, funerals and cemeteries, neighbors would often find Martha roaming the woods at night, howling at the moon. When approached, she would simply stare at them, offering no explanation. Martha's sister told stories of how Martha saw visions and claimed to speak with angels and demons. Martha herself testified that the devil visited her at night while roaming the woods and told her to kill her family. During the trial, she testified to her in-depth conversations with the devil. In a 1930 *Toledo Bee* article, Martha herself stated, "I see ghosts.… Every night they come and sit on the edge of my bed in their grave clothes, they point their fingers at me." Martha had also confessed, during the trial, to burning down three local barns and a church. She was also suspected of poisoning livestock. So we have a woman who talks with the devil, sees ghosts, burned down a church, roams the woods at night howling like a wolf, poisoned seventeen people, murdered three people and allegedly poisoned livestock. Martha would have definitely been perceived as a witch by some in the community.

The most conclusive piece of research connecting Martha Wise to the Witch's Ball and the Stoskopf family has to do with Lily Gienke. If you recall, Lily Gienke was Martha's aunt and one of the three that eventually died due to the arsenic poisoning. Lily Gienke was born Lily Stoskopf. She is the brother of George Stoskopf, who is buried behind the Witch's Ball or the Stoskopf family monument. Lily Gienke, Fred Gienke and Sophie Hasel (three of Martha's victims) are also buried at Myrtle Hill Cemetery—however, nowhere near the Witch's Ball. In 1962, Martha's sentence was commuted by the governor of Ohio. Martha's family wanted nothing to do with her and neither did any local assisted living or nursing homes. With nowhere to go, Martha returned to prison voluntarily and lived there until her death in 1971. She is not buried at Myrtle Hill Cemetery.

When I look into ghostly sightings, I often find that it's the most subtle experiences of witnesses that stand out. For instance, when people visit Myrtle Hill Cemetery, they talk of a mysterious woman dressed in black who appears to be grieving. This mysterious mourner has also been witnessed leaving roses on certain headstones. Given Martha Wise's obsession with funerals, grieving and dressing in black, this mysterious ghostly mourner could be the spirit of Martha roaming the cemetery, mourning for those she killed. If you are ever attending a funeral at Myrtle Hill and you notice a strange, thin woman with a sunken face dressed in black, crying, I suggest you be careful. Oh, and if she offers you water, please don't take it!

On a final note, please allow the Stoskopf family to rest in peace, as they have no connection to the horrible crimes committed by Martha Wise, nor are they associated with any witchcraft. This is simply a case of mistaken identity and exaggerated legends gone wild.

CHAPTER 11

THE GHOSTLY HITCHHIKER OF I-71

Interstate 71 is 343.78 miles and runs from Cleveland through Columbus and Cincinnati, ultimately ending in Louisville, Kentucky. As travelers crisscross this highway, they should be aware that there is a stretch of I-71 between Medina and Brunswick where motorists frequently spot a ghostly hitchhiker. The apparition is seen walking in the northbound lane along the berm, usually between midnight and three in the morning.

In 1993, Rich Heileman, a Cleveland-area journalist, was driving home to Berea from Medina after spending time with friends. He had made this journey many times, was not under the influence of alcohol or drugs and denies being tired or sleepy. Driving north on I-71, just as he crossed over from Medina to Brunswick, he noticed a man walking alone on the side of the road. It was around one in the morning, and Rich believed that the man might be in trouble or, at the very least, need a ride. Rich described the man as being in his thirties, having dark hair and wearing a light tan raincoat and black pants. Slowing down to around twenty-five miles per hour, he made his way toward the stranger. Within three hundred feet, his headlights picked up the man as he turned toward Rich and put out his thumb. Despite having his headlights shining on the man, Rich was unable to make out his face, as it appeared darkened and weirdly blank. As Rich pulled closer, the hitchhiker suddenly became transparent and vanished. Heileman recounts that, shocked and confused, "I pressed the pedal to the floor to get out as fast as I could."

Rich Heileman's account was detailed in Chris Woodyard's book *Haunted Ohio III* and a newspaper article in the early 2000s written by Mr. Heileman himself. Intrigued by the story, I reached out to Mr. Heileman to discuss his experience further. As we talked, he recounted the event exactly as it was described earlier and was gracious enough to answer some additional questions. According to Heileman, the encounter occurred around the change of season from summer to fall. The weather was clear, with nothing out of the ordinary like rain or fog. When asked about the era of the hitchhiker's clothing, he estimated it to be around the 1960s. He based this on the coat the man was wearing, which was a tan, knee-length raincoat with a type of rounded collar that was very popular in the 1960s. He stated that the man did not appear to be in distress, confused or irritable and was simply walking north along the berm. To this day, he has not been able to rationalize the event and continues to seek answers about what might have occurred along that stretch of highway in Medina County. Heileman was not sure of the exact location where the ghostly encounter occurred; however, he stated that it was "right before you leave Medina and enter Brunswick."

The Vanishing or Phantom Hitchhiker is a very common ghostly tale that has been told for hundreds of years around the world (yes, even before cars). As a matter of fact, the Phantom Hitchhiker is considered by some to be

I-71 North just before Brunswick. *Katrina Massullo.*

an urban legend or modern folktale similar to crybaby bridges and Bloody Mary. In 1942, American folklorists Richard Beardsley and Rosalie Hankey collected seventy-nine accounts of encounters with the vanishing hitchhiker from individuals across the United States and published their findings in a series of academic articles in the *California Folklore Quarterly*. According to Beardsley and Hankey, "Many of the ghosts of European folklore haunt roads or places they suffered an accident or misfortune." Beardsley and Hankey identified several different variants of the vanishing hitchhiker story; however, the main structure involves the driver picking up the hitchhiker and then conversing with them or driving them to a location, only to have the hitchhiker mysteriously vanish.

What is really interesting is that a vanishing hitchhiker shows up in the Bible. New Testament Acts 8:26–39 tells the story of the apostle Phillip and an Ethiopian. Phillip was instructed by an angel to travel south on a road from Jerusalem to Gaza, whereupon he came across an Ethiopian man riding in a chariot. The angel instructed Phillip to chase down the chariot. As Phillip was running alongside the chariot, he noticed that the man was reading Isaiah the Prophet's teachings. They struck up a conversation, and the man invited him into the chariot. During their conversation, Phillip essentially converted the man to Christianity, and as they passed a body of water, the man asked to be baptized. They stopped the chariot, and the man was taken down to the body of water and baptized. As soon as the Ethiopian man came out of the water, Phillip mysteriously vanished, and the man never saw him again. According to scripture, Phillip was taken away by the same angel, as it appears his task of converting the Ethiopian to Christianity was complete. From the perspective of the Ethiopian man, he met a stranger and gave him a ride in his carriage, then the man simply vanished, which is strikingly similar to most accounts of the folklore of the vanishing hitchhiker.

What is interesting about Rich Heileman's encounter on I-71 is that it does not fit nicely into the typical vanishing hitchhiker lore. Most accounts involve the driver picking up the hitchhiker and conversing with them to some degree until they ultimately vanish. In Heileman's case, the spectral hitchhiker vanished before Heileman even stopped his car. I could not locate anything regarding a fatal accident or missing person near the area where I believe Heileman saw the spectral hitchhiker; however, Heileman noted that shortly after the event, he spoke with a journalist friend who conveyed that he was aware of many eyewitness accounts of this spectral hitchhiker along this stretch of haunted highway.

CHAPTER 12
THE HOUSE BUILT ON A TOMB

Lodi is the "city of firsts" in Medina County. Lodi, which was originally called Harrisville, was formed in 1811 and is the oldest settlement in Medina County. Lodi was also the site of the first hospital, first organized church, first organized cemetery, first documented birth and first election in Medina County. Judd Leatherman was the first Eagle Scout in Medina County, and Maggie Leatherman Hershberger was the first to take the Iowa Test of Basic Skills in Medina County. Lodi was also very progressive, as it was home to the first female mortician (Edith Elliot) and female judge (Elizabeth Winters) in Ohio. Dr. Henry Mabry delivered and raised the smallest palomino horse in the world in Lodi. Miss Fancy was born in 1952 and was twenty-two pounds and twenty-three inches long. Adorable. Lodi is also home to the first and only house in Medina County built on an ancient sacrificial tomb. Not adorable.

In 1824, Joseph Harris built his third residence in Lodi on what is now the corner of Ainsworth and Harris Streets. The house was torn down in the 1960s, and currently, a bank, the Lodi Police Department and the village offices are located in its general vicinity. Before we get into the ancient tomb lying under your local bank, let's get to know Lodi's founding father, Joseph Harris, a little better.

Joseph Harris (1782–1893) is the founding father of Lodi. He was born in Connecticut; however, in 1801, at the age of nineteen, he traveled over five hundred miles west and settled in Randolph, Ohio (Portage County). By

Harris House, 1960s. *Courtesy of the Lodi Historical Society.*

1810, he was working as a surveyor for the Torringford Land Company and was married to Rachel (Sears) Harris (1792–1874); they had a son, Albert Harris (1808–1897).

The Connecticut Western Reserve was a portion of land in northeastern Ohio claimed by the Colony of Connecticut under the terms of a charter with King Charles II in 1662. Connecticut lost claim to some of its western lands following the American Revolutionary War; however, it did retain ownership of the eastern portion of its land, which included what would become the counties of Ashtabula, Cuyahoga, Erie, Huron, Geauga, Lake, Lorain, Medina, Portage, Trumbull, Ashland, Mahoning, Ottawa, Summit and Wayne. Much of the land often called the Western Reserve was sold to a group of investors who formed the Connecticut Land Company. The Connecticut Land Company would survey the land and then sell portions of it to early settlers. The land that would become Lodi was called Township No. 1, in Range 16, and was composed of roughly two thousand acres. A group of sixteen investors who called themselves the Torringford Land Company bought Township No. 1 in Range 16 and then selected Harris to be the land agent for this township, with the task of selling off one-hundred-acre parcels to early settlers. In exchange for his services, Harris was deeded two hundred acres of property.

In 1810, armed with only an axe, Joseph Harris left his house in Randolph, Ohio, and headed fifty miles west to settle what would become Lodi. Along the way, he encountered many dangers, including a furious bear who growled and lunged at Harris. Harris did not heed the advice I was always given, which was to remain still around bears, and instead charged the bear. Luckily, the bear wasn't looking to fight and instead walked away. Harris's first impression is described in *History of Medina County*:

> *The flickering light of the setting sun was dancing and glowing through the rustling leaves of stately trees. With the awe-inspiring impression of the grand sight before him, the resolution formed that he would make this his future home.*

Harris's first residence was constructed on flat marshland with dense alder trees, bogs and cranberry bushes. The first official residence in Lodi was more like a log hut than a home, as it had no door, only a small opening several feet off the ground for him and his family to crawl through. This was done to keep the dangerous wildlife out and the heat in. The Harrises' first house is located on what is now the corner of High and Prospect Streets. Once land was available to purchase, settlers slowly moved to the area and built residences, and a government was created, which officially named the town Harrisville (after Joseph Harris). Due to ongoing issues with their mail being mixed up with that of Harrison County in Ohio, the townspeople of Harrisville held a meeting to determine a new town name. It's not quite clear if Lodi was named after a city in Italy or if it was given its name because it was located on the *low di*vide of Medina County. Joseph Harris built his second home on the corner of Wooster and Market Streets. The Harrises' third residence was, of course, built in 1824 on the corner of Ainsworth and Harris Streets—unknowingly on top of an ancient tomb constructed by a prehistoric culture called the Mound Builders.

The Mound Builders roamed parts of America from 1500 BCE through 1751 CE. This culture got its name from the numerous earthen mounds it constructed for religious,

Joseph Harris, from *History of Medina County, 1881.*

ceremonial, burial and residential purposes. Ohio has seventy preserved Mound Builder sites that are open to the public. The most famous site is the Serpent Mound in Chillocothe, which is 1,370 feet long and shaped like a curved snake. The site is believed to have been built by the people of the Adena culture, which flourished between 500 BCE and 100 BCE. Exact numbers are impossible to know, but estimates are that the Adena Culture had around eight to seventeen million inhabitants spread throughout present-day Ohio, Indiana, Kentucky and West Virginia. The Adena culture is named after the estate where artifacts were first discovered in Adena, Ohio. Theories abounded in the late 1800s and early 1900s regarding what race or culture constructed the mounds. Some believed these mysterious Mound Builders were descendants of Vikings, Hebrews, Africans, Chinese or Greeks. Others suggested that the mounds were so unique and advanced that they were possibly built by the displaced inhabitants of Atlantis. The most likely answer is that the builders were ancestors of Native Americans.

So why build these mounds, and what the heck is in them? Some mounds were constructed as effigies to local animals; however, a majority were burial sites for people held in high regard. Temples were often built on top of these burial mounds, where ceremonies and rituals were performed.

The Harris house was built on a mound that was 160 feet (east to west) by 135 feet (north to south) and 12 feet high. While excavating in the cellar, workers discovered the remains of nine human skeletons of "large" stature. According to reports, the skulls were big enough to fit over the heads and rest on the shoulders of early settlers. The teeth in these ancient skulls were described as "doubled all the way around." The arrangement of the skeletons in the tomb was odd as well, according to Joseph Harris's son, Albert: "It looked as if the bodies had been dumped in the ditch. Some of them had been buried deeper than others, the lower one being about 7 feet below the surface." Along with the skeletal remains, the workers also found a stone altar made of cobblestones arranged in a circle, with charcoal and ashes possibly from a sacrificial feast. This monument or altar was nine feet below the surface. Additional renovations in 1869 uncovered an additional two skeletons. While not much is known about the Mound Builders' culture, there is some speculation that they sacrificed humans and animals. The spiritual leader of the Mound Builders was referred to as the Great Sun. Upon the death of a Great Sun, some of his spouses and servants, believing it was their duty, accompanied the deceased into the afterlife. While some thought it an honor to sacrifice themselves, others were unwilling and were drugged, killed and then placed next to their ruler. This might explain the odd arrangements of the bodies noted by Albert Harris, as those sacrificed for the Great Sun were in fact "dumped" into the grave, while the Great Sun was buried deeper next to the altar.

While it might seem unsettling to live atop an ancient tomb, by all accounts, the Harrises didn't seem to mind. In a 1949 article, Maude Harris, who would have been the fifth generation of Harrises to live in the house, stated she was "not in the least perturbed." According to Maude, the discovery of bones was not that uncommon: "The last time we remodeled the house, workers dug up some more bones but we merely found them interesting and kept them on exhibition for a while." The bones were exhibited by the family due to the town's curiosity and the bones' unusually large size; however, their current location is unknown.

If there are going to be restless spirits, angry ghosts or poltergeist activity, this location should definitely be a hot spot; however, oddly, it's not. The generations of Harrises who lived in the house never reported any paranormal occurrences, at least not publicly. According to Letha Mapes, president of the Lodi-Harrisville Historical Society, there have been occasional reports of phantom footsteps in the village offices, which are located on the property of the former Harris House. Several years ago, a paranormal investigation team witnessed some unusual phenomena and collected some ghostly evidence while taking pictures inside the village offices; however, other than that, this location is deadly quiet.

CHAPTER 13

WAITE-HARRIS HOUSE

The Lodi-Harrisville Historical Society is currently located at 111 Harris Street in a house called the Waite-Harris House. The house was built in 1890 and is named after its original owners, Dr. James E. Waite (1853–1928) and his wife, Rachel Harris-Waite (1862–1940). The Waite-Harris house is located directly across from Joseph Harris's third residence (which is currently a bank and was an ancient sacrificial tomb). Walking into the Waite-Harris House is like stepping back in time: original woodwork, built-in bookcases, original fireplace, pocket doors and a swinging service door. I took a seat in the parlor surrounded by ornate original woodwork, historical Lodi memorabilia, historical documents and period clothes worn by previous Lodi residents to talk ghosts with Letha Mapes, who is the president of the Lodi-Harrisville Historical Society. Letha is extremely passionate about Lodi's history, even the haunted kind. She has heard many stories from the previous residents and renters who once lived in the house prior to the historical society moving in.

The basement seems to be the area where people feel most uneasy. Previous residents have reported a sensed presence and overwhelming emotions there on numerous occasions. Overwhelming emotions are often associated with ghostly encounters: for example, walking into a room and getting an intense feeling of sadness or anger for no apparent reason. Ghostly encounters are also believed to trigger overwhelming somatic or physical symptoms, such as nausea, shortness of breath, tingling sensations, headaches, overwhelming fatigue or dizziness. Sudden changes in one's emotional and physical state

Waite-Harris House, 2021. *Brandon Massullo.*

could be a concern for anyone, especially if they believe it's triggered by a discarnate entity.

A previous resident who lived in the house for a number of years reported that as he was leaving the basement and ascending the stairs, he distinctly felt someone grab his shirt and attempt to pull him back down into the darkness. As we have discovered throughout this book, staircases seem to be a hot spot for paranormal encounters. Several psychics and paranormal investigators have visited the house, and the consensus is that a spirit remains. According to Letha, one psychic got very pale and clammy upon entering the basement, stating, "Yes, there is something down here." When Sonya Horstman (Psychic Sonja), who is a local psychic and often guides ghost tours in Medina County, was visiting the Waite-Harris House, she reported the basement has "powerful" amounts of "psychic energy" and sensed the presence of a woman. Sensed presences, shadow people and overwhelming emotions with no apparent trigger are frequent phenomena reported throughout the house by different individuals across several decades.

A grand piano once graced the parlor of the house. A previous resident reported an odd experience one night in which she had an overwhelming urge to play to the piano, almost as if compelled by an invisible force. While playing, she had an intense feeling of love, and as she turned her head, she

Basement stairs, Waite-Harris House, where a ghost was reported to have grabbed a former resident. *Brandon Massullo.*

Basement, Waite-Harris House. *Brandon Massullo.*

witnessed an apparition of a man watching her play. Oddly enough, she was not frightened, and she continued to play until the ghost simply vanished. It seems as if this location has a wide range of phenomena, so let's take a look into its history.

Dr. James E. Waite graduated from medical school in 1882 and shortly after moved to Lodi, where he began to practice medicine. Along with being a physician, Waite owned and ran a ninety-acre farm in Westfield Township, served as the director and president of the Lodi State Bank, was the director of the Farmers Insurance Company and was president of the board of directors of the Lodi Hospital. On October 25, 1883, Dr. Waite married Rachel Harris, who was the daughter of Nelson Harris and great-granddaughter of Lodi's founding father, Joseph Harris. Rachel Harris was a noted artist and musician who had a studio in the house. The Waites had two children, Harris Waite (1885–1973) and Mary Faye Waite-Thompson (1888–1918). Dr. Waite passed away at home after a surgery in 1928. Rachel remained in the home until her death in 1940. At that time, her son, Harris, moved from Akron and lived in the home until his death

Parlor where a piano was located and the apparition of a man was witnessed, Waite-Harris House. *Brandon Massullo.*

in 1973. The house had five owners from 1973 until it was bought and turned into the historical society. Some of those owners lived in the house, and others rented it out.

The haunt-type phenomena reported in the Waite-Harris house are very pure and have not been tainted by people speculating about the identity of the ghosts and their possible motivations for haunting the location. "Pure" might seem like an odd word to use when describing a haunting, but as I have mentioned in previous chapters, it's best to focus on the experiences themselves. Here we have consistent phenomena (sensed presence, overwhelming feelings without a trigger, tactile phenomena and apparitions) happening to numerous individuals over several decades. If you get a chance, please visit or even join the Lodi-Harrisville Historical Society, and as an added benefit of joining, you might get a free ghostly experience.

I debated whether to add this last paragraph for several months; however, I want to be honest when it comes to ghostly encounters. I have been studying the paranormal for over twenty years. I studied parapsychology at the University of Edinburgh in Scotland, where I completed my dissertation on "Environmental Sensitivity and Paranormal Experiences," which included a five-day scientific experiment in one of Scotland's most haunted locations, Mary King's Close. I spent several hours alone in Scotland's most haunted location, with no ghostly phenomena occurring. I have been to numerous reportedly haunted locations throughout the world and have never experienced an apparition, odd noise, sensed presence, shadow person or unexplained cold spot. In other words, I have never had a ghostly encounter or spine-tingling experience…until the Waite-Harris House in Lodi.

While taking pictures in the basement, I experienced both auditory and tactile phenomena. I distinctly heard a woman whisper "Hello" in my ear, as if she was inches way. I even felt her breath. I stood motionless as a rush of emotions and thoughts bombarded me. I carried on taking the pictures and exploring the basement, hoping for another interaction; however, nothing else occurred. This moment replays in my head on a daily basis. Could I have been mistaken? Did this really happen? Is there a rational explanation? I've argued with myself for hours about whether this was natural or supernatural and currently have no definitive answers. I've traveled the world researching ghosts, only to possibly encounter one ten minutes from my house. Lodi is definitely the city of firsts!

CHAPTER 14
SHARON TOWNSHIP'S FIRST SCHOOLHOUSE

Around the year 1816, the families of Abram Valland, Lyman Green, Charles McFarlin, David Holmes, David Point and the Tuffs, the Parameters and the McConkeys moved into the area that would become Sharon Township. The land was primarily used as a hunting ground for the men in neighboring Wadsworth and Medina. The owners of the land were Samuel Mather and Richard Hart, who purchased the land through the Connecticut Land Company. They paid $26,087 for a total of 16,139 acres and, although the name was not official, called the land Mather's Town. In 1828, the land was officially surveyed, and in 1831, a township was formed, and property was able to be purchased. With the formation of a township, a proper name was given to the land, which was "Gash." This name was so unpopular that it only lasted three months until it was changed to Sharon. Sharon Township was a melting pot of early settlers, with a colony of Pennsylvania Dutch and a village of English miners. The group of immigrants who came directly from England settled in the northwest part of the township and gave their neighborhood the name of English Settlement.

In the fall of 1822, a town meeting was held among the early squatters of what would become Sharon Township. The topic to be discussed was the location of the town's first schoolhouse. The site chosen was in the vicinity of what is now called Coddingville, which had in those times a reputation for large rattlesnakes. Rattlesnakes were often mistaken for large trees lying across the roads—until, of course, the tree slithered away. In fact, a large snakeskin was found in the woods near Coddingville that was sixteen to eighteen feet long. A local resident hung it on his porch, and visitors would travel to admire it. The location for the schoolhouse was quite controversial, which led to objections from some of those present during the meeting. According to *History of Medina County* (1881), a young Native American woman had been buried at the proposed site only a few years previously. The young woman's spirit was said to have been both seen and heard at the site since discussions had started about building the schoolhouse over her final resting place. The spirit was said to have been pleading with the settlers to let her bones lie in peace. "I do not want the place where my bones lie disturbed. Why is my sleep disturbed? Who is it call the dead?" The spirit also told of the wrongs perpetrated against her people by the early settlers, who stole land, broke promises and introduced the Native Americans to the poison of whiskey. Unfortunately, the young Native American's ghostly pleas went unheeded, and the schoolhouse was quickly erected on her grave.

The early settlers spared no expense on the schoolhouse, and it was said to be better than the majority of schoolhouses at that time. The floor, desks and stools were all made of split chestnut logs. The teacher's chair was made of elm.

The exact location of Sharon's first schoolhouse has been lost to time. The only passage regarding its location can be found in a book written in 1881 called *History of Medina County*, which states the schoolhouse once stood

Possible location of Sharon's first schoolhouse, in the vicinity of Dunsha and Route 18. *Katrina Massullo.*

where Link's Tavern stood in 1881. Link's Tavern was owned by G.B. Link, who owned property on both the Sharon and Granger sides of what is now Route 18. I talked with local historian Mike McCann about the location of the schoolhouse, and we suspect that it most likely was in the vicinity of Route 18 and Dunsha Road (on the Sharon side); however, since the schoolhouse was erected prior to Sharon being officially surveyed and a township formed, it is possible the school actually resided on the Granger side of Route 18 and Dunsha.

CHAPTER 15

THE FARMER WHO COULD DODGE BULLETS

An article in the February 18, 1921 *Medina Sentinel* is titled "The Haunted House at Sharon Is Sold: Lonely Landmark Is Said to Be Spirit Rendezvous." The house that was reportedly a hot spot for spirits was owned by John P. Beech (1853–1920), a wealthy and influential farmer in Sharon Township. After Mr. Beech's death in March 1920, the home stood unoccupied and was in disrepair. Stories of ghosts walking through the home circulated throughout the neighborhood. Many witnesses reported seeing ghosts moving around the house restlessly, as if searching for something. Others noted that the spirits were playful and would often be seen frolicking through the home. Those who dared to venture close to the house reported ghostly noises and sounds of chains rattling. Children and adults alike were said to avoid the house at all costs. One Sharon resident stated that he heard stories of more nefarious things occurring at the Beech farm, such as animal sacrifices and cults. It's clear that the Beech farm had a reputation throughout the county of being haunted; however, are these just tales, or is there some truth to them? Let's get to know John Beech a little more and see if we can uncover the origins of these stories.

Mr. Beech never married and by all accounts lived alone on four hundred acres. He died at the age of sixty-six from a heart attack while working in a barn on his property. In Ensworth and Morris's *Sharon Vignettes*, John Beech was described as a tall man with great strength and a strong will. He was also noted to be a shrewd bargainer who had penchant for acquiring land. It was said that he would purchase more land and livestock than he could adequately care for. While Mr. Beech was a prominent farmer, he appeared to have a dark side.

John Beech was brought to trial and convicted on two occasions of cruelty to animals. The first case occurred in 1912 and attracted a great deal of attention in the surrounding rural communities. Reporters, neighbors and people interested in the latest scandals flocked to the courtroom in Medina. It was said that the trial was the hottest ticket in town. In the course of the two-day trial, twenty-four witnesses were called to the stand. The testimonies were quite gruesome, as humane agents reported finding numerous dead sheep lying frozen to the ground on Beech's property. The agents also reported that they found live sheep in Beech's basement that were too weak to even stand. No water or food was found, and the veterinarian who examined the sheep determined they died of malnourishment. The estimated number of dead or dying sheep was close to one hundred. Due to the sheer amount of evidence (including photographs), Mr. Beech was convicted.

In the winter of 1916, Mr. Beech was again charged with animal cruelty. In this case, he was accused of not providing adequate shelter for his cattle. Humane officers testified that over one hundred of Mr. Beech's cattle suffered from lack of food and shelter, which led to several cattle dying needlessly. During the trial, Samuel C. Anderson, who worked part-time for Mr. Beech, testified that the cattle were well cared for and treated humanely. Mr. Anderson was well-respected in the community and a devoted father and husband. Despite Mr. Anderson's testimony, John Beech was again convicted of animal cruelty; however, he was not sentenced to jail, perhaps due in part to prominent businessmen testifying on his behalf. Shortly after the trial, Mr. Anderson and Mr. Beech had an argument over money and severed ties. Anderson went on to work for the Ohio Match Company of Wadsworth and appeared to be moving on with his life. Looks can be deceiving, as Anderson was silently ruminating on the money owed to him by Mr. Beech.

On a cold December morning in 1917, Anderson, upset due to never having been paid money owed to him by Beech and recently having his buggy repossessed by Beech, got extremely angry. Anderson stormed off to Beech's property and confronted him. Anderson pulled out a .32-caliber revolver and, while standing within ten feet of Beech, unloaded the chamber. All was quiet, and as the smoke settled, Beech stood unharmed and not fazed in the slightest. Beech shouted several insults toward Anderson and then calmly walked away. Surprisingly, Beech did not contact the police; however, Anderson walked straight to the police department and turned himself in.

SHOT SIX TIMES

Though Only Ten Feet Away Missed Each Time.

Sam Anderson of Sharon Township Shoots at John Beech, His Former Associate.

Beech headline, 1916. *Courtesy of the Medina County Gazette.*

During the trial of Samuel Anderson, more details regarding his motive for the attempted murder came to light. Anderson reported that Beech owed him several hundred dollars for hiding evidence (burying dead cattle) and lying in court. Anderson essentially recanted his testimony in Beech's defense during the animal cruelty trial, stating that Beech did not care for his animals and they would often die of starvation or thirst or simply freeze to death. In a statement, Samuel Anderson declared, "I'm willing to go to hell if I can have John Beech there beside me."

Following the trial, Beech regaled the crowd with an explanation of how he dodged six bullets. He claimed that his instincts were so sharp that he ducked just prior to Anderson shooting. Beech claimed that Anderson had a tell and that prior to pulling the trigger, he would wink. Anderson's tell may have helped Beech escape death that day.

It would seem that the stories of animal sacrifice do have some basis in truth. While Beech was never accused of sacrificing animals or belonging to a cult, he was convicted on two occasions of animal cruelty. Also, according to newspaper accounts, many animals died needlessly under Beech's care on the property. One can see how, over time, the accounts of animal cruelty and death could morph or get exaggerated into sacrifice. The exact location of John Beech's house has been lost to time. Records indicate his house was demolished soon after its purchase in the 1920s, and much of his four hundred acres has been parceled off and sold to different people in the past one hundred years. As far as I can tell, his property was about one mile west of Sharon Center. If any Medina County residents find themselves in that area, be sure to look for the ruins of the Beech farm—but be careful, because bullets are useless against ghosts, especially ones with the skill to dodge them.

CHAPTER 16

THE MEDIUM BURIED UNDER THE KITCHEN DOOR

F ixler Road in Sharon Township is five miles long and spans the entire
length of Sharon Township, east to west. It's a typical rural Ohio
road with a mixture of fields, farms and houses; however, it was once
reported to be the epicenter of spiritualism in Medina County. Spiritualism
is a religious movement that peaked in the late nineteenth century and is
based on the belief that spirits, departed souls or ghosts can communicate
with the living through mediumship. Mediums, or spirit mediums, are
often confused with psychics. Psychics claim to have the ability to gather
information through telepathy, extrasensory perception (ESP), precognition
or clairvoyance. Most psychics don't get this information from the deceased,
spirits or ghosts but rather through paranormal abilities like "reading the
mind" of an individual or seeing into the future. Mediums, on the other
hand, act as a conduit between the world of the living and the dead. They
communicate directly with the deceased through channeling, physical
phenomena (objects floating, ectoplasm, spirit manifestations, etcetera) or
Ouija boards. These communications often occur in the context of a séance.

In the late 1800s, spiritualist camps, where believers gathered to connect
with and talk to the dead, were widespread throughout Ohio. Spiritualism
was widely accepted by Ohioans; therefore, it wasn't weird to have friends
over on the weekend to hold a séance and attempt to contact deceased
relatives. Séances were so common that they even occurred in the White
House; Mary Todd Lincoln attempted to contact the spirit of her eleven-
year-old son, who died of fever in 1862. Ohio is considered by some

researchers to actually be the birthplace of the Ouija board or, as it was called in the spiritualist camps in Ohio, the talking board. The talking board was the precursor to the Ouija board. It was similar in design and included a board with letters, numbers and a planchette-like device for the spirit to communicate through. The talking board was not mass-produced or patented, and each was individualized by the medium or spiritualist who created it. In 1890, a group of businessmen (who were not spiritualists) looking to capitalize on the popularity of spiritualism and the talking board patented their board, named it the Ouija board and marketed it to families all over the world. The popular game manufacturer Parker Brothers bought the rights to the Ouija board in 1966, and at one point it outsold Monopoly.

According to Medina legend, a very gifted medium named Charlotte "Lottie" Bader lived in Sharon Township. Lottie was a teenager who lived with her parents in a home on Fixler Road. The Bader house soon became headquarters for séances, which quickly resulted in Lottie's fame and celebrity spreading throughout the county. The Baders shared a property line with the Warretts, a wealthy family who were often in conflicts with the Baders. In April 1845, a mysterious fire burned the Warretts' house to the ground. There were no clues regarding the cause of the fire; however, the Warretts had strong suspicions that Lottie and her father knew more about the fire than they disclosed. Lottie held a séance shortly after the fire, in which she claimed that the fire was started by the ghost of a former employee of the Warretts.

Ten or so years after the fire, Lottie became ill and soon discontinued her séances. She made an odd request to her mother: if she should die, she wanted to be buried near her parents' kitchen door so she could visit them often. Not long after her request, on a dark and stormy night, Lottie died. The legend states that moments before her death, Lottie asked her mother to bring her tea and toast. When Mrs. Bader went to prepare the tea and toast, she witnessed an apparition of a headless woman, who told her, "This you will have to do once a week the rest of your days." Upon returning to Lottie to give her the tea and toast, her mother found her dead. After Lottie's death, she was buried, per her request, under the doorway to the kitchen. The Friday after her burial, Mrs. Bader was awakened by footsteps on the kitchen floor. Startled, she asked, "Who's there?" The voice of her daughter, Lottie, responded, "Mother, I am hungry. Can you make me tea and get me something to eat?" Mrs. Bader hurried to the kitchen and found nobody there. Perhaps she believed that she had dreamed the event, so she returned to her room, where she again heard the ghostly voice of Lottie: "Put it on the table, Mother, and go back to bed." Mrs. Bader made the food and tea, placed it on the table and returned to bed. When she awoke the next morning, the food had been eaten. Mrs. Bader prepared Lottie's meal every Friday for the next five years until Mrs. Bader's death. Mr. Bader continued to live in the house until his death. Lottie's body was eventually removed from its grave under the kitchen doorway and reburied in a cemetery on a hilltop in Sharon Township. The headstone is said to read: "Charlotte Bader, died July 24, 1858, aged 25 years."

Of all the stories I unearthed while researching the haunted lore of Medina County, I have to say that this one is by far the most fascinating. Can you imagine preparing tea and toast for your daughter's ghost every Friday night for five years? Would you be able to literally walk over your daughter's corpse every time you left your house? Could you eat meals every day knowing that your daughter was buried right underneath your feet? These are rhetorical questions, so please don't email me the answers. This story has all the markings of a great ghostly tale: mediumship, a ghost that burns down houses, a woman buried under a house and the weekly return of a young female spirit for tea and toast. It almost seems too good to be true.

I came across the most detailed account of this legend in the book *Early Sharon Township*, which was written by Ruth Ensworth and Helen Vaughn. Both authors were members of the Sharon Heritage Society and tremendous researchers who wrote extensively on early Sharon Township history. In the book, there are two grainy pictures of the Bader house. The house was in disrepair when the photos were taken in 1981 and has since been demolished. In a newspaper article several years later in the *Columbus Citizen-Journal*, Ruth Ensworth noted that she had spoken to the most recent occupants of the Bader house, who commented that ghostly noises remained for whoever occupied the home.

It seemed as if this legend had a solid foundation, so I began my research, trying to verify that Charlotte "Lottie" Bader, her parents and their neighbors the Warretts existed. I thought this would be a slam dunk due to actual photographs of the house, the noted location of the house on Fixler Road and several written accounts of a headstone in a Sharon Township cemetery that read "Charlotte Bader, died July 24, 1858, aged 25 years." I searched cemetery records, census records and other historical records in Sharon Township for the surname Bader and could find nothing. There were also no records of their neighbors the Warretts. Also, there is no grave for Charlotte Bader in any Sharon Township cemetery.

A good researcher never quits…so I quit. I wrote up what I could and chose to move on to the next ghost in Medina County. As luck would have it, I stumbled across Mike McCann, a cemetery historian and researcher who runs a website called MedinaCountyGraves.com. McCann has been preserving burial records through documentation in Medina County since 1996. Turns out that McCann had "McCracked" the mysterious case of Lottie Bader years ago; however, he was too busy hanging out in cemeteries to write up an article for his website. McCann is a cemetery detective who prefers to stick to the facts. According to McCann:

While I appreciate a good ghost story; I want to make sure that they have a historically rooted—and verifiable—base. The Lottie Bader legend was an early one that I ran into and I very quickly discovered that it reeked of bogus lip service lore. My interest was based on the grave aspect. If she was originally buried on her parents' property that was notable as a former burial site in Medina County and I wanted to record her current grave location since no tombstone record existed. Whether you ignore or accept the ghost story, the burial of a daughter by her parents on private property and later moved to a township cemetery is certainly plausible and one that occurred with some degree of regularity back in the 1800s when burial on the family farm was very much legal and normal. The legend is recounted in a book called Haunted Ohio and it mentions how her grave was moved to the township cemetery on the hilltop. Sharon Township cemetery is not on a hilltop and no such cemetery in Sharon Township exists that matches that description. It states that her tombstone reads: "Charlotte 'Lottie' Bader, died July 24, 1858, aged 25 years." No tombstone with that has been recorded or located ANYWHERE. I have seen the official cemetery records for Sharon Township and read the tombstones for that entire cemetery. NOTHING. No Baders or Warretts anywhere. Where did this story come from? I can't trace its roots to anything although I did find one interesting tidbit. In Sharon Township Cemetery is a headstone of interest. "Charlotte B. Brockway, wife of Orlando P., died July 24, 1858, aged 25 yrs." This is not a coincidence. This woman is buried in Section B, Lot 62 of Sharon Township Cemetery on the lot of her father, Edward B. Bentley. She married Orlando on January 21, 1858 and the 1859 atlas map of Sharon Township shows that E.B. Bentley owns pretty much all of Sharon Township Lot 58 which is on the north side of…you guessed it, Fixler Rd.

By all accounts, Charlotte "Lottie" Bader never existed. The Baders and their neighbors the Warretts also never existed or lived on Fixler Road. Thanks to McCann's research, we do know that Charlotte Broadway's tombstone inscription is almost identical to the alleged inscription on Charlotte "Lottie" Bader's nonexistent tombstone of legend, going so far as to have the same dates of death and age. It would seem likely that the true identity of Charlotte "Lottie" Bader is in fact Charlotte Broadway. We also know that Charlotte Broadway was born Charlotte Bentley and that her parents were Edward B. Bentley (1794–1874) and Clerimond Bentley (1799–1874), who lived on Fixler Road around 1857, which was the timeframe mentioned in the Lottie Bader legend.

Edward Bentley built his home on Fixler Road in 1841, and their neighbors to the north were the Walls. According to the 1859 atlas map of Sharon Township, the property belonged to Christian Wall and his family. Is it a stretch to assume that the Walls were the real-life Warretts? Well, they both have surnames beginning with the letter *W*; however, this isn't really sufficient in my opinion. One aspect of the legend of Lottie Bader involved her neighbor's house being mysteriously burned down. Lottie blamed the fire on the ghost of a former farmhand of the Warretts; however, the Warretts suspected the Baders. Turns out that part of the Walls' house and their barn was in fact destroyed in a matter of hours by—you guessed it, a cyclone. No fire, just a terrible tornado that occurred in April 1890. The cyclone of 1890 ripped through Sharon Township, destroying many homes and businesses as well as killing humans and livestock. Christian Wall's farmhouse and barn were mostly destroyed. According to the April 10, 1890 edition of the *Medina County Record*, "Christian Wall's barn was down with all the livestock inside.…Christian Wall's house was severely tried with every building around it being blown down." Does this mean the Walls are the Warretts? Definitely not, but if legends are based in some truth, we do have a lot of circumstantial evidence.

So, what is truth and what is legend? It's really hard to tell. I suppose it's possible that at some point there were families with the surnames Bader and Warrett that lived in Sharon Township. Perhaps they were not born there, never owned property there, did not die there and somehow eluded the census reports. It was fairly common for property owners to rent or lease their land and farms in effort to maximize their profits. Owning several farms that are tended to by families who maintain the property and livestock seems like a sustainable business plan. I could not find any proof that the Bentleys and Walls did not get along or that there was any feud. I also could not find any information on the life of Charlotte Broadway, with the exception of the fact that she married Orlando Broadway in January 1858 and died seven months later in July 1858. Nowhere was it noted that she was a medium or spiritualist. Orlando Broadway is a bit of a mystery as well, as he is not buried next to his wife, Charlotte, or anywhere else in Medina County. Also, it's weird that Charlotte died seven months after they were married. If the Bentleys are the real-life Baders and the Walls are the real-life Warretts, why the names were changed is also a mystery.

This is simply the beginning of researching the haunted lore of Lottie Bader, and I encourage all those interested to take the information provided by myself and Mike McCann and do your own digging. Perhaps someday someone will figure this out.

CHAPTER 17
CRYBABY BRIDGES ON ABBEYVILLE ROAD

The most pervasive urban legend in Ohio is that of the "crybaby bridge." This is an urban legend that revolves around hearing the ghostly cries of a baby around or underneath a bridge. There are over thirty locations that are described as crybaby bridges in Ohio (possibly more). We will look further into the origins of this urban legend later; however, first let's look at Medina County's crybaby bridges.

Medina County is the location of three crybaby bridges, and they are all on Abbeyville Road.

ABBEYVILLE RAILROAD TRESTLE BRIDGE

The Abbeyville Railroad Trestle Bridge is located in the 2300 block of Abbeyville Road just north of Zion Evangelical Lutheran Church and cemetery. This church was organized in 1830, and its congregation held services at different locations, including a log schoolhouse and a framed structure half a mile south of Liverpool Center. Its present location was built in 1894, and the church itself is quite lovely.

Legend states that in the 1920s, a satanic cult once practiced in the surrounding woods, often breaking into the church to perform rituals. As the story goes, during these rituals, they would need to sacrifice a living creature.

Zion Lutheran Church, 2021. *Katrina Massullo.*

Not having an animal to sacrifice, they stole a newborn baby from a local woman and tied the crying baby to the train tracks on the bridge. The cult returned the next day and found the remains of the baby. It is said that, no matter day or night, one can still hear the cries of the innocent baby that lost its life over one hundred years ago. Another variation to this story occurred in the 1980s and states the satanic cult did not tie the baby to the tracks but rather threw it off the bridge; therefore, the ghostly cries come from underneath the bridge.

In order to better understand the history of the Abbeyville Railroad Trestle Bridge, I thought it would be best to start with the history of the railroad in Liverpool Township. The Liverpool Township Historical Society is, oddly enough, housed in the original train depot that was built in 1895. The depot was moved from its original location one mile east in 1976 during a bicentennial celebration. I settled down in this historical train depot and spoke with Rod Knight, who is a member of the Liverpool Historical Society and is very knowledgeable about the history of the railroad in Liverpool Township. Rod moved to Liverpool Township in 1975, and he recalls the bicentennial celebrations, which included the opening of the depot museum and, most, notably the great tug-of-war contest of Liverpool Township. Residents who lived east of the Rocky

River took their positions on one side of the river, and those who lived west took their positions on the other side of the river. It was a glorious tug-of-war battle on that hot and humid July day; ultimately, the losers fell into the river and were soaked in defeat. Which side was victorious? Well, I suggest you stop by the historical society and talk with Rod or perhaps wait for a book to be written about that glorious day.

Let's get back to the railroad. Prior to 1895, trains carrying coal and other supplies would be transported directly from Wheeling, West Virginia, to Black River Harbor in Lorain, Ohio. Coal was essential for making steel and therefore in high demand in Lorain and Cleveland-area steel mills. Once in Lorain, the coal and supplies would then head to Cleveland. It seems that the people running the steel mills in Cleveland didn't like waiting, so it was decided to build a fork in the line with one line heading to Lorain and another line heading to Cleveland. Construction began in 1893 by the Cleveland, Lorain and Wheeling Railroad (CL&W) to create an additional line that would branch off in the Medina County area with the ability to either head to Cleveland or Lorain. After careful consideration, the CL&W Railroad decided to create this fork in the railroad line in Medina County's own Lester, Ohio. Wait. Where is Lester? Lester is actually Liverpool, Ohio.

Abbeyville Railroad Trestle Bridge, 2021. The ghostly cries of a baby are reported to be heard underneath and on top of this bridge. *Katrina Massullo.*

Liverpool Township depot, early 1900s. *Courtesy of Liverpool Historical Society.*

Wait. Where is Liverpool, Ohio? Liverpool, Ohio, is actually Valley City, Ohio. I could keep going if you like, but we'll stop there. Early railroad maps note that the depot is located at the "Lester" intersection; however, nobody exactly knows where the name "Lester" originated. At the time, Liverpool, Ohio, actually existed; however, it had to change its name due to issues with mail. It turns out that East Liverpool's mail kept ending up in Liverpool, Ohio, so it was forced to change its name to Valley City. I wonder how much wrongly delivered mail it takes to force a city to change its name? The line began operating in 1895 in both directions, carrying passengers, mail, coal and other supplies, such as milk. Having a depot in your town was very important, as it brought jobs and businesses (stores, lodging, etcetera) and made travel easier.

Ownership of this specific line changed hands a couple times as usage gradually declined due to improved roadways and increased use of cars and trucks to haul supplies. In 1968, the Liverpool depot closed. Many tragedies, deaths, train wrecks and accidents occurred on this specific line but nothing of note in the Liverpool Township area or specifically along the railroad trestle bridge over Abbeyville Road. In 1925, a train carrying a group of five hundred men, women and children from a Dutch Reformed church in Cleveland was returning home from a day at Chippewa Lake Amusement Park when it encountered the aftereffects of a significant tornado that

Abbeyville Railroad Trestle Bridge, early 1900s. *Courtesy of the Liverpool Historical Society.*

had flooded the Rocky River, damaging and flooding a nearby bridge in Liverpool Township. Somehow, the train made it over the severely damaged bridge and cruised into the depot safely.

In my research, I could find no indication that any infants were killed on or near the Abbeyville Railroad Trestle Bridge. As for the secret satanic cults operating in the woods near Zion Lutheran Church…who knows? I guess if they were a secret cult, no newspapers or historical databases would have known they existed. I reached out to the Zion Lutheran Church to clarify, discuss how this urban legend has impacted them and perhaps give them a chance to set the record straight; however, they did not respond.

ABBEYVILLE BRIDGE (OVER WATER)

The exact location of the second Abbeyville crybaby bridge is unclear. One possible location is a few yards south of Zion Lutheran Church. I find it odd that Zion Lutheran Church is literally sandwiched between two crybaby bridges. I don't believe this has ever happened in the history of crybaby bridge folklore. Did someone have an issue with this church? It's a very modest bridge over a trickling stream.

Above: Abbeyville crybaby bridge over stream, 2021. *Katrina Massullo.*

Opposite: Abbeyville crybaby bridge over Rocky River, 2021. *Katrina Massullo.*

The other possible location is farther down Abbeyville Road just north of Wolf Road, which would actually place it in York Township. This is a bigger bridge than the other, and it spans the Rocky River.

Legend states that in the 1950s, a young girl had a child out of wedlock. Fearful of disclosing her newborn child to her family as well as of the ridicule and judgment of others, she threw the baby into the river below the Abbeyville bridge. If you visit the bridge during a quiet night, it is said that you can hear the baby's gurgling cries as it drowned.

There is no way to determine when and from whom these stories originated. I searched through the records to see if I could find anything of interest regarding the bridges in Liverpool and York Township; however, I found nothing. Also, I could not find any information indicating an infant had died underneath any bridge.

It's unclear which Abbeyville Road crybaby bridge legend started first; however, when reviewing websites discussing the stories surrounding these bridges, I found that they seem to combine them or mix the stories up. Both of the legends are dangerous, as visiting bridges and railroad tracks at night can lead to horrible accidents or even death. In an article that I found from the late 1990s, a group of high school kids nearly fell off the railroad

bridge as they barely escaped an oncoming train while pursuing these false legends. The bridge is still used by trains day and night, making it a very dangerous place to visit.

It's obvious that the crybaby bridges in Medina County are urban legend; however, where did this urban legend start? Is there any truth to these crybaby bridges? Ken Summers wrote a brilliant article titled "Troubled Waterways: Origins of the Crybaby Bridge Legend." Ken states, "People rarely invent a story entirely from scratch; it's based on something they've heard, seen, or read about. Couldn't this be true of the crybaby bridge? Apparently, it is. Believe it or not, we can find evidence that similar events really have happened." Ken was able to undercover twelve real-life newspaper accounts across the United States and Canada of infants being thrown off bridges. The earliest account occurred in 1886 in Long Beach, New Brunswick (Canada). A four-year-old boy named Richard Tufts carried his neighbor's newborn baby to a nearby bridge and tossed him over. When asked why he did this, Richard replied, "I don't know." The most recent tragedy occurred in 2010, when a man threw his three-month-old child off the Garden State Parkway's Driscoll Bridge in New Jersey. Ken eloquently sums up what we fear the most in this world: "What makes these tales of crybaby bridges so popular isn't just the fact that they deal with mysterious supernatural themes; it's the fact that they remind us of the dangers within humankind."

CONCLUSION

Most cities, towns and villages have tales of haunted houses. As children, we have all been warned to stay away from a certain place due to its ghostly inhabitants or strange occurrences. Have you ever wondered when the first written account of a haunted house was documented? Well, the answer is both complicated and interesting, so let's take a trip back to ancient Greece in the year 194 BCE.

A guy by the name of Plautus, who was a Roman playwright, authored one of the earliest known works of fiction regarding a haunted house. The play was titled *Mostelleria*, which translates from Latin as *The Haunted House*, and is considered to be a main literary source for Roman beliefs about the afterlife before the first century. While the story is fictitious, it gives us a view into early Roman beliefs about haunted houses. In the play, the main character talks of the house being haunted by the ghost of a man who was murdered sixty years earlier. He goes on to say this murdered man was buried on the property. The ghost proclaims that because he was murdered and buried without proper rites, he is doomed to haunt the house.

What can we learn from a play written over two thousand years ago? Since literature is often a reflection of real life, we can to some extent assume that the play is based in some real-life accounts of haunted houses from that period. If this is the case, we can see that the experiences and phenomena in 194 BCE are very similar to modern-day accounts of haunted locations.

Let's look at some common themes in this play, which can be related to accounts of modern-day haunted houses:

- Terrible crime occurred in the house (murder)
- Person murdered was buried on the property (improper burial with no burial rites)
- Murdered person haunts the house (unfinished business, tragedy causes ghost to remain)
- Ghost attempts to communicate crime and tragedy to current inhabitants
- Reports of visual apparitions and auditory phenomena (knocks were reported in the play as well)
- Inhabitants are fearful and scared to live in the house

Plautus most likely took common themes from local stories of haunted locations and incorporated those into his play. Think of modern-day movies about haunted houses such as *The Amityville Horror* and *The Conjuring*. While these movies are exaggerated, they are based on actual events that happened to people living in these reportedly haunted locations. So why do ghosts hang around the living?

Pliny the Younger (61–113 CE) was a lawyer, author and magistrate of ancient Rome. He tells the tale of a house in Athens, Greece, that is so haunted it is uninhabitable. Owners and renters would be driven mad by the ghost that roamed its halls. Sounds of chains rattling echoed throughout the house. The apparition of an old and emaciated man would often appear with chains around his hands and feet. One night, the philosopher Athenodorus stayed at the house. When the ghost appeared, Athenodorus was not scared and proceeded to follow the ghost. The ghost led him to the courtyard and then vanished. Athenodorus marked the spot where the ghost vanished, and the next day, the locals dug at that exact location. At that spot, they uncovered the remains of a man who had chains around his hands and legs. Once the remains were buried properly, the ghost never appeared again. Athenodorus is a ghostbuster, in a sense, because he helped the ghost leave the earthly realm. He did not strap on a proton pack and trap the ghost; however, the end result was the same (i.e., the ghost was no longer bothering people).

One aspect that has changed in modern times is in regard to finding human remains and completing proper burial rites. I've heard occasional accounts from paranormal investigators, TV shows and movies where actual remains are the catalyst of the haunting; however, that is becoming exceeding rare. Modern hauntings focus more on the ghosts having unfinished business, resulting in mediums helping the spirits "cross over"; priests, shamans or demonologists exorcising the negative entities; or paranormal teams "cleansing" or "clearing" the house of the spirits. According to James Van Praagh, who is the author of *Ghosts Among Us*, a producer for the popular TV show *Ghost Whisperer* and a psychic medium, earthbound spirits stay close to earth due to unfinished business, being scared of following the light to heaven or simply because they are confused or unaware of what is going on.

Mediums see themselves as ghost psychologists in that they work with the ghosts or earthbound spirits to determine their issue and help them cross into the light. Van Praagh's views are probably the most commonly held by believers in ghosts or life after death, who adhere to what is commonly called the spiritualist view, which is based on the spiritualism movement in the mid-1800s. Van Praagh did not come up with this theory, as it has been the common hypothesis of ghost hunters, psychics and paranormal enthusiasts for over one hundred years. The idea of ghosts hanging around to complete unfinished business is almost part of our culture. Many TV shows, movies and haunting documentaries use this premise often. The idea is that there is a reason for the haunting, and once that reason is discovered, the ghost or disembodied soul can move on. This notion is perhaps why so much time and effort is spent trying to determine the identity and motives of alleged spirits in a location. There is even a specialization in mediumship called spirit rescue, where mediums are specifically trained in crossing-over techniques and tools to help earthbound spirits. The TV show *Ghost Whisperer*, which Van Praagh produced, has a similar theme in almost every episode, which involves the medium gaining information from the ghost, then working with the ghost to help them find peace and cross over.

Looking back through the haunted stories in Medina County, we can definitely see some ancient haunted themes come to life. The schoolhouse in Sharon Township experienced the ghost of a Native American woman due to building on top of her grave. Improper burial could also be ascribed to the Lottie Bader ghost, as she was buried under the kitchen. The hauntings at Main Street Café were reportedly triggered by throwing away human remains. Rattling chains were heard at the Beech farm. Terrible crimes or tragedies were reported at the Medina Steak House, crybaby bridge, etcetera. Franklin Sylvester seems to have unfinished business with the Medina County Library, perhaps upset that the library is no longer named after him.

Just because a belief is part of pop culture doesn't mean that it's accurate. We are bombarded with TV shows, movies, books and ghost-hunting reality shows that reuse the same old tropes: for instance, a ghost died here tragically and now is destined to haunt this location. Anyone who tries to tell you that there are rules to ghostly encounters or paranormal phenomena is a liar. There are stories of hauntings that occur in newly constructed homes, homes with no history of murder or trauma and even historically peaceful locations. A ghost or haunting is not indicative of tragedy, crime, trauma or evil. I might argue that having a ghost or haunting could be a positive sign. Perhaps the discarnate soul loved the place so much that they choose to hang around. Who is to say that because ghostly phenomena are witnessed on a couple occasions, the ghost is *always* at the location? Perhaps the spirit just pops in occasionally to see how their old house or restaurant is doing? Are we misconstruing a haunting or ghostly encounter as being negative or demonic, when in fact it's a blessing?

In this book, I've attempted to trace the history of local lore and spirits, hoping to find their origins. This led, on occasion, to the discovery that the stories were not accurate or based in history. For example, I noted that the Lady in Blue (Becca Wilcox) never lived in or died at the Hinckley Historical Society; however, who says that ghosts only have to haunt the places that they lived in or died in? I can walk down the street or travel anywhere in the world; why can't a ghost? I would argue that ghosts should be better suited than the living for frequent travel, since they aren't hampered by a physical body, gas prices or walls.

As I have mentioned frequently throughout the book, it's best to focus on the enchanting experiences and ghostly phenomena rather than trying to identify a ghost. If you have been lucky enough to have a life-changing paranormal experience, simply use it to motivate your life and spirituality.

BIBLIOGRAPHY

Beardsley, R., and R. Hankey. "A History of the Vanishing Hitchhiker." *California Folklore Quarterly* 1, no. 4 (1943): 13–25.

———. "The Vanishing Hitchhiker." *California Folklore Quarterly* 2, no. 4 (1942): 303–35.

Belanger, Michelle. *Haunting Experiences: Encounters with the Otherworldly.* Woodbury, MN: Llewellyn Publishing, 2009.

Blanco, Juan Ignacio. "Edward Wayne Edwards." Murderpedia. http://murderpedia.org/male.E/e/edwards-edward.htm.

———. "Martha Wise." Murderpedia. Accessed April 10, 2021. https://murderpedia.org/female.W/w/wise-martha.htm.

Boyer, Sam. "A Popular Haunt." *Medina (OH) Sun Sentinel*, October 29, 1981.

Brown, Gloria. "Haunted Hinckley." *Ohio Libraries* (April 1993), 30–31.

Cassano, Erik. "Ghost on the Loose." *Medina (OH) Gazette,* January 22, 2004.

———. "The Ghost in the Cellar." *Medina (OH) Gazette*, August 18, 2003.

Cavey, Laura. Interview with the author. August 20, 2021.

Cleveland19.com. "Convicted Killer Pleads Guilty to Slaying a Norton Couple in 1977." June 11, 2010. www.cleveland19.com/story/12633629/convicted-killer-pleads-guilty-to-slaying-a-norton-couple-in-1977/.

Cleveland Plain Dealer. " Past and Present of Medina's First Town." February 2, 1930.

Collins, Ken. Interview with the author. June 2021.

Dawidziak, Mark. "Ghost Cashers." *Akron (OH) Beacon Journal*, October 27, 1996.

Dermody, Diane. Email correspondence. May 28, 1998. Medina County Library Reference Records.

———. Personal email. June 4, 1998. Medina County Library Reference Records.

Derrick, Rachel. "Taking a Tour of the Supernatural." *Medina (OH) Sun*, June 26, 2008.

Encyclopedia Britannica. "Salem Witch Trials." Accessed April 10, 2021. https://www.britannica.com/event/Salem-witch-trials.

———. "Spiritualism." Accessed March 14, 2021. https://www.britannica.com/topic/spiritualism-religion.

Encyclopedia of Cleveland History. "Stouffer, Vernon Bigelow." Case Western Reserve University, May 12, 2018. https://case.edu/ech/articles/s/stouffer-vernon-bigelow.

Encyclopedia.com. "The Mound Builders: The Poverty Point, Adena, Hopewell, and Mississippian Cultures." June 16, 2021. https://www.encyclopedia.com/humanities/encyclopedias-almanacs-transcripts-and-maps/mound-builders-poverty-point-adena-hopewell-and-mississippian-cultures.

Ensworth, Ruth, and Dorothy Morris. *Sharon Vignettes Vol. 1*. Sharon, OH: Sharon Township Historical Society, 1992.

Ensworth, Ruth, and Helen Vaughn. *Early Sharon Township*. N.p., 1981.

Felton, D. *Haunted Greece and Rome: Ghost Stories from Classical Antiquity*. Austin: University of Texas Press, 1999.

Finley, Deana. "Real Ohio Haunts." *Cleveland (OH) Plain Dealer*, October 27, 1999.

Gladden, John. "Some Say Spooky Local Legends Aren't Just the Halloween Variety." *Medina (OH) County Gazette*, October 31, 1991.

Glunt, Nick. "What Lies Within the Witch's Grave?" *Medina County (OH) Gazette*, October 26, 2013.

Hambley, Stephen. *Timeline of Medina County History: New Historical Facts*. Ashland, OH: Bookmasters, 2017.

Harrington, Mary. "Fifth Generation of Family of First Arrival Now Prominent in Town." Lodi-Harrisville Historical Society Archives, undated.

Heileman, R. David. "In the Spirit of the Season." *Medina (OH) Gazette*, October 27, 2005.

Heileman, Richard. Interview with the author. July 2021.

Heinke, Ed. "Spooky Tales Pepper Locale's History." *Columbus (OH) Citizen-Journal*, October 29, 1980.

Hyde, Robert. "Medina's Uptown Park or Medina Square." Beyond the Storefronts. Accessed May 15, 2022. http://www.medinasquare.org/uptown-park#uptown-park-medina.

———. "West Liberty Street/North Medina." Beyond the Storefronts. Accessed May 15, 2022. http://www.medinasquare.org/west-liberty-streetnorth#north-west-public-square-landmark.

———. "West Liberty Street South Medina." Beyond the Storefronts. Accessed May 15, 2022. http://www.medinasquare.org/west-liberty-street#west-liberty-south.

———. "West Side of Public Square #13–#21." Beyond the Storefronts. Accessed May 15, 2022. http://www.medinasquare.org/westside-of-square#west-pub-thirteen.

———. "South Broadway Street Medina." Beyond the Storefronts. Accessed May 15, 2022. http://www.medinasquare.org/south-broadway-street-209.

Kachuba, John. *Ghosthunting Ohio*. Cincinnati, OH: Emmis Books, 2004.

King, Joann. *Medina County: Coming of Age 1810–1900*. Cleveland, OH: Self-published, 2016.

Knight, Rod. Interview with the author. June 26, 2021.

Lange, Renese, et al. "Contextual Mediations of Perceptions in Hauntings and Poltergeist-like Experiences." *Perceptual and Motor Skills* 82 (1996): 755–62.

Lodi-Harrisville Historical Society. *Lodi Leads the County!* Lodi: OH: n.d.

Mace, Gina. "Graveyard Visitors Keep Eye on the Polished Granite Ball." *Akron (OH) Beacon Journal*, October 29, 2000.

Mapes, Leetha. Interview with the author. July 1, 2021.

Marino, Brittany. Interview with the author. June 25, 2021.

Massullo, Brandon. *The Ghost Studies: New Perspectives on the Origins of Paranormal Experiences*. Wayne, NJ: Career Press, 2017.

———. "The Earliest Haunted House." Haunted Theories. https://www.hauntedtheories.com/single-post/2019/01/07/the-earliest-haunted-house.

MCDL Genealogy Team. "H.G. Blake." *Medina County District Library Genealogy Blog*, April 26, 2017. http://mcdlgenealogyspot.blogspot.com/2017/04/hg-blake.html.

———. "Haunted Medina County—Lisa Rienerth." *Medina County District Library Genealogy Blog*, October 10, 2017. http://mcdlgenealogyspot.blogspot.com/2017/10/haunted-medina-county-lisa-rienerth.html.

———. "Judge Albert Munson." *Medina County District Library Genealogy Blog*, October 10, 2019. http://mcdlgenealogyspot.blogspot.com/2019/10/judge-albert-munson.html.

McDonell-Parry, Amelia. "Inside One Man's Serial-Killer Unification Theory." *Rolling Stone*, June 25, 2018. www.rollingstone.com/culture/culture-features/inside-one-mans-serial-killer-unification-theory-630621/.

McRobbie, Linda Rodriguez. "The Strange and Mysterious History of the Ouija Board." *Smithsonian*, October 27, 2013. https://www.smithsonianmag.com/history/the-strange-and-mysterious-history-of-the-ouija-board-5860627/.

Medina County Historical Society. *History of Medina County*. Fostoria, OH: Gray Printing Company, 1948.

Medina (OH) County Gazette. "The Beautiful Sylvester Library Now Belongs to the Public." October 4, 1907.

———. "Beech was Found Guilt of Cruelty." April 7, 1916.

———. "Burnham House Not Yet Built." June 10, 1881.

———. "Case Against Beech for Cruelty to Animals." March 31, 1916.

———. "Communication: Letter to the Editor." November 23, 1906.

———. "Death of Captain Austin Badger." November 16, 1883.

———. "Death of Railroad Man at Germania House." April 18, 1895.

———. "Death of Thomas Murphy." March 24, 1898.

———. "Death's Call: Franklin Sylvester Passed from Life Last Friday Morning." June 7, 1907

———. "John Beech Convicted of Cruelty of Animals after Two-Day Trial." March 8, 1912.

———. "Julia Miller Rites Are Held." July 24, 1945.

———. "Killed on the Railroad." October 14, 1881.

———. "Local Items: Woman in Black." November 16, 1906.

———. "Obituary: Edward Burnham Wife and Child." March 24, 1882.

———. "Obituary: Emily Burnham." March 27, 1891

———. "Obituary: Josie Burnham." April 6, 1877

———. "Obituary: Nelson Burnham." March 10, 1882.

———. "Shot Six Times: Sam Anderson of Sharon Township Shoots at John Beech His Former Associate." December 21, 1917.

———. "Thomas Murphy Shot." March 10, 1898.

———. "Weekend Blaze." February 19, 1979.

Medina (OH) Sentinal. "The Haunted House at Sharon Is Sold." February 18, 1921.

———. "Sharon Man Seeks Life of Neighbor." December 21, 1917.

———. "Sudden Death of Fred Curtiss." January 1, 1915.

———. "To Stand Trial for Shooting to Kill." December 28, 1917.

Miller, Pamela. "Ghosthunters Search for Spirits at Cool Beans." *Medina (OH) Post*, January 17, 2010.

Mitchell, Matthew. "3 Haunted Restaurants in Cleveland." *Cleveland Magazine*, October 23, 2018. https://clevelandmagazine.com/food-drink/articles/3-haunted-restaurants-in-cleveland.

Moonspenders. "Troubled Waterways: Origins of the Crybaby Bridge Legend." Week In Weird, September 3, 2011. http://weekinweird.com/2011/09/03/troubled-waterways-origins-crybaby-bridge-legend/.

Moorehead, Karlin. "Ouija Board: The 'Mystifying Oracle' That Outsold Monopoly in 1967." Groovy History, November 29, 2016. https://groovyhistory.com/the-ouija-board-was-so-popular-it-out-sold-monopoly-and-continues-to-be-a-cultural-phenomenom.

Moreman, Christopher. *Beyond the Threshold: Afterlife Beliefs and Experiences in World Religions*. Lanham, MD: Rowan & Littlefield, 2018.

Morrow, Walter. "Weeping Martha Wise Sobs Over Her Three Murders." *Toledo (OH) News-Bee*, November 19, 1930.

Nelson, Ben. "The Devil in Hardscrabble Alley." *American Weekly*, January 4, 1942.

Newsnet5.com. "Ghosts Haunt Hinckley Library." September 8, 2004. Medina County Library Reference Records.

Northrop, N.B. *Pioneer History of Medina County*. Salem, MA: Geo. Higginson Book Company, 1861.

Perrin, William, et al. *History of Medina County and Ohio*. Chicago: Baskin and Battey Historical Publishers, 1881.

Persinger, M. et al., "Experimental Stimulation of Haunt Experiences and Elicitation of Paroxysmal Activity by Transcerebral Complex Magnetic Fields: Induction of a Synthetic Ghost?" *Perceptual and Motor Skills* 90 (2000): 659–74.

Price, Mark. "The Witch's Ball." *Akron (OH) Beacon Journal*, October 27, 2003.

Redmond, Ray. "Pre-Historic Mounds Visible in Medina Area." Lodi-Harrisville Historical Society Archives, undated.

Reinerth, Lisa. Interview with the author. July 31, 2021.

Rhoades, Nikki. "The Darling B&B Just South of Cleveland That's Crazy Haunted." Only in Your State, August 3, 2019. https://www.onlyinyourstate.com/ohio/cleveland/haunted-bb-cle/.

Rodriguez, Cindy. "Librarians Hush Ghost Stories." *Akron (OH) Beacon Journal*, October 28, 1993.

Rose, Mia. Interview with the author. August 1, 2021.

Rose, Ryan. Interview with the author. August 1, 2021.

Sangiacomo, Michael. "Lodi, a Spooky Little Place: Ohio Tiny Towns." October 7, 2018. https://www.cleveland.com/news/erry-2018/10/49204625225320/lodi-a-spooky-little-place-ohi.html.

Schulte, Emma. Interview with the author. April 2021.

Sell, Jill. "Ohio's Ouija Board Connection." *Ohio Magazine*, October 1, 2017. https://www.ohiomagazine.com/ohio-life/article/ohio-s-ouija-board-connection.

Spitzer House Bed and Breakfast. Accessed May 31, 2021. https://spitzer.house/inn/history/.

Vanderschrier, Elaine. Letter correspondence. April 4, 2000. Medina County Library Reference Record.

———. "Strange Sightings at the Library." *Hinckley (OH) Record*, October 1993.

Webb, Criag. "Books Will Check Out; 2 Ghosts May Remain." *Akron (OH) Beacon Journal*, October 31, 2003.

Webber, A.R. *History of Hinckley*. Elyria. N.p., OH: 1933. Reference Book, Medina County Library.

Webster, Jim. "Haunted: Spooky Spots in Medina County Lore." *Medina County (OH) Gazette*, October 26, 2002.

Workman, Paul. "Hinckley Library Was Once Home to the Vanderschriers." *Medina County (OH) Gazette*, April 17, 1997.

Wikipedia. "Mound Builders." Accessed July 3, 2021. https://en.wikipedia.org/wiki/Mound_Builders

———. "Stouffer's." Accessed April 12, 2021. https://en.wikipedia.org/wiki/Stouffer%27s.

———. "Vanishing Hitchhiker." Accessed July 23, 2021. https://en.wikipedia.org/wiki/Vanishing_hitchhiker.

———. "Vernon Stouffer." Accessed April 12, 2021. https://en.wikipedia.org/wiki/Vernon_Stouffer#cite_note-5.

Willis, James A. "Abbeyville Road Bridge." *My Strange & Spooky World* (blog), February 2020. http://strangeandspookyworld.com/crybaby-bridge-project/abbeyville-road-bridge.

Wiseman, R., et al., "An Investigation into the Alleged Haunting of Hampton Court Palace: Psychological Variables and Magnetic Fields." *Journal of Parapsychology* 66 (2002): 387–408.

Woodyard, Chris. *Haunted Ohio*. Dayton, OH: Kestrel, 1991.

———. *Haunted Ohio III*. Dayton, OH: Kestrel, 1994.

———. *Haunted Ohio IV*. Dayton, OH: Kestrel, 1997.

About the Author

Brandon Massullo is a clinical therapist, author and parapsychologist residing in Medina, Ohio. He has graduate degrees in clinical counseling from the University of Toledo and in psychological research methods from the University of Edinburgh in Scotland. His research at the University of Edinburgh centered on electromagnetic fields (EMFs) and ghostly encounters, and he studied within the Koestler Parapsychology Unit. Brandon has been fascinated by paranormal phenomena for twenty years and has been a participant and featured speaker in numerous paranormal forums and events, including *Coast to Coast AM* and the Parapsychological Association's sixtieth anniversary celebration. His research has been cited in parapsychological journals, newspaper articles and mainstream books. Please visit Brandon at Hauntedtheories.com or on Facebook or Twitter (Haunted Theories) for more research into ghosts, apparitions and all things paranormal.